FLASHING BLADES

FLASHING BLADES

The Story of British Ice Hockey

Phil Drackett

 The Crowood Press

First published in 1987 by
The Crowood Press
Ramsbury, Marlborough
Wiltshire SN8 2HE

British Library Cataloguing in Publication Data

Drackett, Phil
    Flashing blades: the story of British
    ice hockey.
    1. Hockey – Great Britain – History
    I. Title
    796.96′2′0941   GV848.4.G7

    ISBN 1 85223 061 4

This book is dedicated to Réné Francis Galbraith 'Bobby'
Giddens, who devoted his life to the cause of ice hockey in
Great Britain, and to all the others I met along the way.

Typeset by Acorn Bookwork, Salisbury, Wiltshire
Printed in Great Britain,
at the University Printing House, Oxford

Contents

Forewords

This history of more than one hundred years of British ice hockey is more than welcome. There have been books in the past recording the game in general, together with individual team handbooks and instruction manuals, but here we have the story of ice hockey in this country from its early beginnings in the Fens up to the present day.

Phil Drackett is well qualified to write such a story. His knowledge and love of the sport have been evident both before and after the Second World War, and his ability as a specialist ice hockey journalist was appreciated by all. I first met him in 1946 at Harringay Arena, when I was Secretary of Brighton Tigers Ice Hockey Club.

With the recent resurgence of ice hockey in Britain, this historical record of the game will be of great interest, not only to the new generations seeing ice hockey in its current form, but also to the old-timers who can browse through memories of great games and players of yester-year.

ALAN WEEKS

When 'Sandy' Archer asked me to leave Winnipeg in 1946 to join a new team in England, Nottingham Panthers, I little dreamt that Nottingham would become my permanent home. Over the years there have been some great moments: when Panthers won the English National League in 1951 and 1954, and when I played with the Wembley Lions team which won the British League in 1957, and perhaps none better than when hockey returned to Nottingham in 1980.

After forty years in British ice hockey (apart from brief spells back in Canada and in Switzerland and five years in Sweden) I am delighted that at last a history of the game in this country is being published.

I first met Phil Drackett in my initial season in England. Later he accompanied the Panthers on tour, and on a number of occasions I played for All Star teams organised by Phil and his long-time partner, 'Bobby' Giddens. More recently, we have worked together in promoting our favourite sport.

I am sure that *Flashing Blades* will be compulsive reading for everyone who loves the game.

LES STRONGMAN

When Phil Drackett approached me to write a foreword to this book, my memories were drawn back to the countless personalities and players who contributed in their own way to the making of British ice hockey.

Sir Arthur Elvin who had the vision to stage the sport at Wembley in the 1930s and bring it to a vast new audience; the 'Icy' Smith family who kept the game active in the North; 'Bobby' Giddens who edited *Ice Hockey World*; 'Red' Stapleford who brought hundreds of Canadian ice hockey players to these shores; 'Bunny' Ahearne, the BIHA and World Ice Hockey President; Alan Weeks of BBC Television; and the famous players who in their own right were household names.

We can now see once again the revival of the sport in the 1980s. Television will bring it into our homes. New ice rinks will be built in more and more cities, and the number of teams will expand the League. New stars and personalities will emerge and take over the mantle of the old to help keep alive the glories and thrills of one of the world's most exciting sports.

GEORGE BEACH

Acknowledgements

Memories of more than fifty years along the Great Ice Way are distilled in these pages, but since time tends to reshape the events of yester-year I am much indebted for the recollections and opinions of many great players. They have not only given of their time, but have often loaned precious cuttings and photographs. Especially do I thank Carl Erhardt (and his son, Phil), Ernie Ramus, George Shaw, John 'Lou' Bates, Clarence 'Sonny' Rost, 'Jo-Jo' Grabowski, Henry Hayes, Gerry Heffernan, Charlie Sumner, Grace Sumner, Don Cumming, Arthur Green, George Beach, Les Anning, Les Strongman, Stu Cruickshank, Harry Todd, Mike Daski and TV commentator Alan Weeks. I have had great assistance from British Ice Hockey Association President and Secretary Fred Meredith and Pat Marsh and from the Norwich Union Insurance Group. Thanks also to Arthur Barker Ltd for permission to use an extract from *Bob Bowman on the Ice*.

Bound volumes of *Ice Hockey World* and *Ice Hockey World Annual* have refreshed my memory, and 'Peter' Patton's book *Ice Hockey* (Routledge, 1936) was invaluable in researching the years before my time. My thanks also to Stewart Roberts whose *Ice Hockey Annual* filled in the gaps when I was away from the game in the 1970s.

Any mistakes are mine.

PHOTO ACKNOWLEDGEMENTS

Thanks are due to the following: BBC, Bill Smith, Brighton & Hove Gazette, Douglas Avent, Evening Argus (Brighton), Francis Page, Frederic Holland, GRA, Glynn Goodson, George Fish, Gainsborough Pictures, High Density Plastics, Hilton Photographics, James R. Smith, Lee, Peerless Photography, Picture Press, Roger Fell, Samuel Preval, Sport & General, Wembley Stadium, W.J. Bayliss, W. Stout, Michael Taylor, Jean Bayes, and the Norwich Union Insurance Group.

1 COLD NIGHT IN GARMISCH

A torrent of words, all in an unfamiliar Canadian accent, was pouring from the big old Pye radio in the corner of the room where a man and two boys huddled, drinking in every colourful phrase and expression:

'The score is still nothing-nothing in this match between Great Britain and the United States of America. We're in the second overtime period – eighty minutes of hockey and still no goal has been scored. Erhardt, the British captain, is taking the puck down the ice now. He's skating fast and he's at the American defence, but he's been side-tracked into a corner and he can't get his shot away. Both teams are piling into the corner to get that puck and there's a great scramble going on. There's a left hook to the body and a right-cross to the jaw. Fists and sticks are flying everywhere.

'No, no, ladies and gentlemen, this is not a re-broadcast of the Petersen–Neusel fight. This is just a broadcast of an ice hockey match between Great Britain and the United States of America, being played during the Winter Olympic Sports at Garmisch-Partenkirchen.'

Then the BBC faded out. There were howls of rage from the three grouped around the Pye, howls which were echoed in hundreds of homes all over the British Isles. For the date was 15 February 1936, and on the result of that match depended the outcome of the Olympic, World and European Ice Hockey Championships.

To be fair to the BBC, the commentary had already overrun by three-quarters of an hour, a piano recital had been scrapped and the news was late.

The uproar made front-page news. The BBC had six hundred telephone calls and a stack of telegrams and letters. The commentator, Bob Bowman, previously a humble sub in the BBC's Empire News department (although he had broadcast a Winnipeg Monarchs' game in 1934–35) became famous overnight and was signed-up by the *Daily Express* as a featured sports columnist. And the great British public suddenly became aware that there was a sport called ice hockey.

Great Britain held on through three overtime periods to a 0–0 draw, Canada then defeated the Americans, and Great Britain became the first team to win the Triple Crown of Olympic, World and European Championships. This was to launch an ice hockey boom which would survive the Second

World War and last until the 1950s.

In a way, the story had begun with a decision of the British Ice Hockey Association that all English National League teams should have at least four British-born players, one of whom had been in the country for at least two years, and should also include a player who had played for one or more years in English hockey. Teams anxious to attract good quality players went to Canada seeking puck-chasers who had learned their hockey there but had been born somewhere in the British Isles. Trouble was to result from this, of which more later.

In the 1934–35 season, the British team had narrowly missed the European Championship, playing-off with the Swiss for the title and losing 1–0 on a disputed goal. Canada, represented by the powerful Winnipeg Monarchs, had taken the world title.

Now, with a host of good British-born hockey players to choose from, Vassar Hunter, President of the BIHA and a former hockey player himself, and 'Bunny' Ahearne, the shrewd Irish Secretary, saw a great chance for Britain to do even better. They also believed they had the right man to handle the team – P.H. (Percy) Nicklin, who had master-minded Moncton Hawks to two Allan Cup victories in Canada and was, in the season of 1935–36, to coach Richmond Hawks in the English National League, as well as give some guidance to the newly-formed Brighton Tigers.

First the national team had to be chosen. There was almost a glut of goalminders. Nicklin himself had brought over Moncton's goalie, Jimmy Foster, to play at Richmond; Wembley Lions had 'Scottie' Milne and Art Child; 'Jock' Riddell was with Kensington Corinthians; and there were several others playing minor hockey, including George Mason, Queens, who was reckoned to be the best of the British born-and-bred netmen at the time; Bill Lane, of the near-League strength Birmingham Maple Leafs, who had played senior hockey in Canada; and Streatham's reserve goalie, Stan Fitchett.

Streatham had a host of players who could qualify for Britain, including past internationals Carl Erhardt, Gerry Davey, Pete Halford, Ernie Ramus and Ralph Couldrey, and two new Canadian-reared players, Ernie 'Al' Batson, who could play defence or forward, and Archie Stinchcombe, a forward.

Wembley's eligible contingent included Gordon Dailley, another who could play on the blue-line or up-front; and forwards Alec Archer and Jack Kilpatrick. There were also a couple of Army officers qualified by residence, Carr and Lane. Both had already played for England, and Carr had been captain on occasions.

In addition to Foster, Richmond's candidates included a former international from Manchester, Neville Melland, and two hard-working forwards, Edgar 'Chirp' Brenchley and Johnny Coward, both imports.

Earls Court Rangers and Kensington Corinthians could offer Riddell, defencemen 'Scotty' McAlpine and Paul MacPhail, and forwards Jimmy Chappell, 'Scotty' Cameron and Jimmy Shannon.

Brighton had two good contenders in Harry Pyefinch and Jimmy Borland, and again there were some useful players outside the League, men like Manchester and England forward G. Hewlett Johnson and Birmingham player-manager Sid Bissett. Even the colourful former captain of Great Britain, Blane Sexton, was still performing for Queens.

To help the selectors, a series of Test Matches was arranged between England and Canada (represented by Canadians playing in the League). The British team then chosen was:

Jimmy 'The Parson' Foster, Richmond Hawks (goal). Born Glasgow, Scotland, 13 September 1907. Learned hockey in Winnipeg. Contemplated entering the Church at one time, hence his nickname. Four years with Moncton Hawks (twice Allan Cup winners), during which missed only one of 220 games the team played, saving an estimated 6,000 shots. Foster was the first goalie to register two straight shut-outs in Allan Cup finals, 2–0 and 3–0 against Saskatoon Quakers in the 1931–32 season, and he held the Canadian record of playing for 417 minutes without being scored upon. There was a strong case for suggesting that he was the best goalie in the world at that time, at least outside the professional ranks. He enhanced that reputation in the 1936 Olympics and was to go on to more great days with Richmond Hawks, Harringay Greyhounds, Glace Bay Miners and Quebec Aces. Remarkable for a man who broke his leg in two places in 1930 and was warned he might not be able to play again.

Arthur 'Art' Child, Wembley Lions (goal). Born England, 1916. Weight 161lb. Learned hockey in Canada where he played for Guelph City. Something of a surprise choice; 'Bobby' Giddens, player-coach of Kensington Corinthians, reckoned 'Jock' Riddell should have got the job, but the latter's chances probably disappeared in a deluge of rubber as the hapless Corinthians nosedived towards the bottom of the League. Child was to have a somewhat up-and-down career in hockey and at one time played with a commercial outfit, Perivale Rovers (Philco Radio), for whom two other sometime seniors, Norm McQuade and 'Red' Thomson, also played. After his retirement

Jimmy Foster; Britain built their Olympic hopes around the man described as the world's greatest goalminder.

Carl Erhardt; a veteran of 39 when he led the British team to the Triple Crown.

Bob Wyman; speed-skating champion who became a regular on defence for Great Britain.

from the game, Child became a Member of the Canadian Parliament.

Carl Erhardt, Streatham (defence and captain). Born Beckenham, Kent, England, 15 February 1897. At the time of the 1936 Olympics, Erhardt was already a veteran of 39. He learned his hockey at school in Switzerland and Germany, and afterwards played with Princes, and he led Great Britain in the 1934–35 Championships. Despite his years, Erhardt was strong, fit and awkward to pass. He wrote a book, *Ice Hockey*, and continued as a senior administrator of the British Ice Hockey Association for many years after his retirement.

Robert Wyman, Wembley Canadians (defence). Born London, England, 1913. Twenty-three years of age at the time of the Olympics, Wyman was chunky but small for a defenceman, weighing only 148lb. However, he was exceptionally fast – not surprising as he was a British speed-skating champion before he turned to hockey. A hold-over from the 1934–35 British team, he later played in the English National League with Richmond Hawks, Harringay Greyhounds, Streatham and, in the first post-war season, with Wembley Lions. He also turned out with Queens.

Gerry Davey, Streatham (right-wing). Born Barking, England, 1914. Another member of the 1934–35 team, Davey had over 100 international caps despite his youth, first pulling on an English sweater at the age of sixteen. Many references give his birthplace as Port Arthur, Ontario, but Gerry told the present writer that he was born in England. The family emigrated to Canada, but his mother decided to return home when Gerry was in his teens. Whatever the arguments over his birthplace, he also qualified for Great Britain by residence. Davey was to have a long and distinguished career in British hockey, eventually playing and coaching in the burgeoning Scottish League. He and Carl Erhardt were close, playing together with Princes and Queens Club before moving on to Streatham.

Jimmy Chappell, Earls Court Rangers (centre or wing). Born Huddersfield, Yorkshire, England, 25 March 1915, but taken to Canada at the age of 10. Played with Oshawa Collegiates, Ontario scholastic champions; Oshawa Seniors; and Whitley, Ontario intermediate champions. A good footballer and, like many a Yorkshireman, an outstanding cricketer who was later to play in first-class cricket with the Canada national side.

Gordon Dailley, Wembley Lions (defence or left-wing). Is listed in some reference books as born and educated in England, but hailed from Calgary, Alberta. However, like Davey, he qualified for Great Britain anyway under the residential rules then applying. He played for Grosvenor House Canadians in 1933, and in 1934, when he was chosen for the British team in the World and European Championships, he signed for Wembley Lions. Big and fast, this versatile player was equally at home in defence or attack. He was a Major in the Canadian Army during the Second World War, stayed on in peacetime, and as Colonel Dailley was a Canadian representative on the Korean Armistice Commission.

Alec 'Sandy' Archer, Wembley Lions (right-wing). Born in West Ham, London, England, 1911. Weight 156lb. Fast skater who, after Bobby Walton's departure, teamed with the brothers Tony (centre) and Bert (left-wing) Lemay to give Lions one of the most powerful lines in the history of British hockey. Archer was also an outstanding soccer player. A quiet, thoughtful man who believed in scientific methods, he was later to be coach at Wembley, Nottingham and Murrayfield.

Jimmy Borland, Brighton Tigers (centre or defence). Borland's versatility probably earned him his selection over his hard-hitting team-mate, defenceman Harry Pyefinche, who impressed many experts in the England v. Canada Test Matches, held as trials before the selection of the British team. The burly Borland had been out of the game for a season, but prior to that had teamed with Gordon Dailley on the blue-line for Grosvenor House Canadians.

Jack Kilpatrick, Wembley Lions (left-wing). At 17 the youngest member of the team, this 156lb forward earned selection after some sound performances in the Test Matches and in the face of a considerable challenge from players like Jimmy Shannon.

Edgar 'Chirp' Brenchley, Richmond Hawks (right-wing or centre). Born London, England. Learned his hockey in Niagara Falls, later moved to Harringay with Nicklin, where he played for the Greyhounds.

Johnny 'Red' Coward, Richmond Hawks (left-wing). Not much of a scorer, but a tough hardworking two-way forward who earned his selection.

Arthur 'Archie' Stinchcombe, Streatham (left-wing). Although selected as a left-winger, this versatile player also appeared at centre and played some of his career in British hockey on right-wing. Born at Cudworth, near Barnsley, Yorkshire, the 170lb forward was 23 at the time of his selection, having impressed the powers that be after only a few weeks in English League hockey. Previously he had played with Windsor Mic-Macs, Ontario Hockey Association champions, alongside 'Red' Stapleford, and then with Falconbridge Miners, where a

Archie Stinchcombe; Streatham star who played a major role in Britain's triumph.

The ice rink at Garmisch, high in the Bavarian Alps, where ice hockey history was made.

team-mate was 'Babe' Donnelly. All three were to play with Streatham. Stinchcombe later became coach of Nottingham Panthers and, at the time of writing, is still resident in that city.

These, then, were the thirteen selected to carry the Union Jack in Germany. Of the more notable omissions, Wembley Canadians' captain, Jimmy Carr, was posted to Egypt before the Olympics.

The two Scottish-born Rangers' defencemen, McAlpine and MacPhail, were probably thought to be too big a risk. McAlpine's vigorous style had been inhibited by strict English refereeing and, in any case, he had earlier toured Europe with the Toronto Sea Fleas when they represented Canada in the World Championship so that, Scottish-born or not, his presence on the Great Britain squad would almost certainly have been protested by Canada. MacPhail spent much of the season in the penalty-box, and after being in a free-for-all with half the Wembley Lions confessed that he was afraid the fracas would cost him his international place. He was right, it did.

The English National League contributed two other players to the Olympics. Baron 'Dickie' von Trauttenberg, Streatham defenceman, was to captain Austria, and Jimmy Haggarty, Wembley Canadians' centre, was co-opted by Canada.

The Canadian practice had been to send their Allan Cup winners to represent the country, but the 1935 winners, Halifax Wolverines, had disbanded. Port Arthur Bearcats were chosen instead and they decided to recruit Haggarty who had played for them the previous season, although they did not take another Wembley player, Sammy Gigliotti, who had also played in 1934–35. Montreal Royals protested against the choice of Port Arthur and eventually their captain, Ottawa's Ralph St Germain, was added to the squad.

The twin villages of Garmisch and Partenkirchen lie at the foot of the Zugspitze, Germany's highest peak, and the Olympic Ice Stadium there had been officially opened on 17 November 1935, when 4,000 spectators saw a Berlin Select draw 1–1 with a Bavarian Select. However, there were 20,000 in the stands as 28 nations marched past Adolph Hitler at the Games' opening ceremony. There was great public interest in Australia's one-man team – Ken Kennedy, British speed-skating champion and a hockey player with Birmingham Maple Leafs.

Before a game could be played, the international body decided to uphold the suspension by the Canadian Amateur Hockey Association of 16 English National League players. Two of them, Foster and Archer, were key members of the Olympic team. The Canadians claimed that the players had not obtained permission to play in England. In Foster's case there was even a suggestion that as Moncton Hawks had played against a Detroit team, he was a Canadian international and so not able to play for his home country. After a great deal of discussion some sense prevailed, and President Gilroy, of the CAHA, agreed to lift the suspension for the period of the Olympics. However, that was not to end the behind-the-scenes ructions.

Fortunately the British team did not let the bickering get them down. For the first time they had a top-class coach, a man who really knew what he was doing, and under his direction the team had settled down happily. Captain Carl Erhardt described them as 'a happy family' and he was including Vassar Hunter, Ahearne and Nicklin in that 'family' as well as the thirteen players.

Great Britain were drawn in a pool with Sweden and Japan, thus avoiding the stronger nations and giving them a good chance of reaching the next round. Just the same, the Swedes, although not the hockey power they later became, were no push-overs, while the Japanese had first visited Europe for the World Championships as long ago as the 1929–30 season. On that occasion they also played in London, losing 7–1 to England and 4–3 to Cambridge University.

Britain met Sweden first, and Nicklin iced Foster in goal, Erhardt and Borland on defence, Brenchley centering Archer and Kilpatrick on one line and Chappell between Davey and

Dailley on the other. The ice conditions were bad, and both teams resorted to long shots. With only three minutes gone Brenchley fired one from behind the blue-line and caught the Swedish minder by surprise, and Britain were ecstatic when, from the face-off, Brenchley got the puck to Archer, the right-winger laid one on Kilpatrick's stick and the young Lion bulged the rigging. Alas, the referee ruled Archer offside.

It wasn't a great game. Both teams were feeling their way and the poor ice didn't help. The Swedes took play to the British rearguard in the second period and that 1−0 lead looked very precarious, only good work by Foster preventing an equaliser.

In the final period, the Swedes were penalised twice in rapid succession but Britain continued to play it tight in the Nicklin tradition of 'what we have, we hold'. This looked like the right policy when the versatile Gordon Dailley, playing on the wing, took a pass from the equally versatile Borland and beat the Swedish goalie all ends up, only to see the puck cleared off the line by a Swedish defenceman. The Swedes pressed desperately for an equaliser in the closing five minutes and their weight advantage gave them an edge, but Foster and his team-mates managed to hold out for a narrow win.

The second match, against Japan, seemed to be easier, but in fact it was closer than the score-line of 3−0 in Britain's favour indicated. Nicklin brought in the small but aggressive Wyman to partner Erhardt on defence, but left himself with some options by using Borland as well as Dailley in the attack. Chappell, Davey and Kilpatrick were rested, and Coward and Stinchcombe played their first games of the tournament.

Following Brenchley's idea in the first match, Archer tried a long shot right at the start and it nearly came off – Homma, the Japanese goalie, juggling the puck like a hot potato before it was finally cleared.

Britain launched attack after attack and nearly paid the penalty for their all-out offensive when the Japanese broke away and Shoji, uncovered in front of Foster, just missed. At the ten-minute mark, Brenchley picked up a loose puck around the net, drew Homma out and put his team ahead. Two minutes later 'Sandy' Archer put them further ahead, his backhand shot going into the net off the goalminder's arm.

The second period started with another British foray, and only a great save by Homma prevented Brenchley, through on his own, adding to the tally. The Japanese retaliated and Foster had to pad away Shoji's shot, but for the rest of the period play was rarely out of the Japanese end and their goal often seemed to bear a charmed life.

A penalty to Wyman in the third period gave the Japanese a chance, but the British wingers were back-checking well and the defence usually took care of the puck-carrier. When the puck-carrier did escape their attentions, the poker-faced Foster was there to outguess him. This time it was the Japanese who were the lighter team and when they tired towards the end, Brighton's Jimmy Borland broke away to make it 3–0 and take Great Britain into the next round.

Sweden also qualified from this pool by beating Japan 2–0.

In Pool A, Canada beat Latvia, Poland and Austria, and the latter also qualified by beating Latvia and Poland.

There were shocks in Pool B where the outsiders, Italy, defeated the strongly-fancied American team 2–1, but the Italians could not repeat their performance against Germany and Switzerland. The Swiss were also much fancied but they lost to both Germany and the USA. The Americans scrambled home 1–0 against the Germans and so both, with one defeat apiece, qualified for the semi-finals, and Switzerland and Italy were eliminated.

Hungary and Czechoslovakia qualified from Pool C, France and Belgium going out. The poor Belgians lost all three of their games, conceding 20 goals and only scoring 4.

Great Britain was drawn in semi-final Pool A, along with Canada, Hungary and Germany. The first match was to be against Canada, and Nicklin put out what he considered his most effective line-up: Foster in goal; Erhardt and Dailley on defence; and Chappell, Davey, Coward, Brenchley, Archer and Stinchcombe up-front.

Davey got out of a sick-bed to play and to the astonishment of a crowd of 10,000 gave Britain the lead 40 seconds from the start – with a long shot. Not even the Canadians had got wise to this little ploy of the devious British.

Chappell and Davey tested the Canadian goalie, diminutive Jakie Nash (later to play for Wembley Monarchs), right from the first whistle, and at the 40 second mark Davey did the unexpected. He picked up a loose puck at centre-ice and, while the Canadians waited to see what he was going to do, he let fly with a powerful flick of the wrist. A little goal-judge waved his flag (no red lights then) in the cold air of a Bavarian evening and the mighty Canadians were trailing by one goal.

The stage was set for a titanic struggle. With Erhardt playing a captain's game and Dailley a tower of strength alongside him, the British lads played like men inspired. It was end-to-end stuff with the British forwards back-checking like mad and stopping the Canucks from running wild. The blow fell at 13.40 of the first period when Ralph St Germain, the man from Montreal, came in off the corner to score from close-in, the first goal Jimmy Foster had conceded in the tournament. The crowd settled back to see a rout: 'Now the Canadians will slaughter them,' they said. Erhardt and his team-mates had other ideas. Gamely, they held out until the interval.

The Canadians came out for the second period stimulated by the inevitable dressing-room pep talk and they forced their opponents back on to the defensive. But the British had all the hallmarks of a Nicklin-coached team, with the forwards skating both ways. Chappell was particularly outstanding, time and again skating opponents into the corner and frustrating the build-up to dangerous moves.

Erhardt and Dailley were blocking well, but much was owed to Foster who was at his brilliant best. His goaltending rose to dizzy heights as he outguessed the Canadian sharpshooters and coolly turned away bullet-like drives, the rhythmic motion of his jaws as he chewed gum being the only sign of emotion. The crowd was in a constant turmoil of excitement, but when the period ended the score was still 1−1.

Canada decided the time had come to stop the nonsense and in the final period they were on the attack throughout. St Germain, Murray, Thompson, Haggarty and Deacon were all right in on Foster in turn, but the Richmond goalminder could not be beaten. Britain were outclassed, but there was nothing wrong with their fighting spirit and they stuck grimly to their task.

Then, with less than two minutes left, the unbelievable happened. Gordon Dailley broke up a Canadian attack, found himself in the clear and made a dash for the opposition goal. 'Chirp' Brenchley, ever a wily one, was quick to see the chance and skated furiously after the big Wembley defenceman to give him support. Dailley let fly as soon as he got within range, Nash padded the shot away − and Brenchley raced in to sink the rebound. Great Britain 2, Canada 1.

There were 90 seconds left, time enough for the Canadians to pepper Foster with four or five shots, but the goalie wasn't changing his parsimonious habits at this stage and gave nothing away. The victorious team filed to the dressing-room down a passageway lined with cheering spectators.

In the dressing-room Erhardt, who had campaigned so long and so hard in Britain's interests, sat in stunned disbelief. It just would not sink in that his team, hoping to have an outside chance at the European title, had beaten the might of Canada. Nicklin, who had not earned the title 'The Iron Man' lightly, a man not given to loquacity, said it all with 'I'm proud of you, boys.' There were some keen observers who swore 'The Iron Man' was near to tears.

At this point the politicians intervened again. Now their team had been beaten, the Canadian Amateur Hockey Association wanted to alter the rule which said that in the finals teams would not have to meet teams they had already beaten in the competition. They were supported by the Germans who saw the prospect of lucrative gate receipts if, for example, Great Britain played Canada again. However, it was pointed out that the rule was identical with previous championships and that the procedure had been carefully explained to officials of all competing nations before the Games began. The matter was put to the vote and Canada and Germany were overwhelmingly defeated.

Britain still had to play Germany and Hungary in the semis and, sensing the danger (the Germans on home ice were proving a handful), Nicklin put out the same line-up as against Canada. In a fast clean game, Gerry Davey scored in the second period, but the Germans tied it up before the end, and three periods of overtime failed to break the deadlock.

On the next day, Britain won a dull game against Hungary without breaking sweat. Davey (2), Brenchley, Chappell and Archer all scored in a 5−1 victory. Meanwhile, Canada beat Germany 6−2 and Hungary 15−0 to go through to the final with Great Britain.

In the other semi-final, the United States topped the pool with wins over Sweden, Czechoslovakia and Austria, and the Czechs accompanied them into the final by virtue of defeating Sweden and Austria. 'Dickie' von Trauttenberg's team came close to qualifying, only losing to USA and Sweden by a single goal.

Under the rule to which the Canadians had objected Great Britain did not have to meet Canada again in the final, nor did the USA have to play Czechoslovakia.

The first match in the final was between Great Britain and Czechoslovakia, with the Championship of Europe hanging on it. Britain relied upon the 'old brigade' of Foster, Erhardt, Dailley, Chappell, Davey, Coward, Brenchley, Archer and Stinchcombe, and it proved to be 'no contest', the Czechs going down 5−0 in one of the cleanest games of the tournament, only one man being sent off throughout. The irrepressible Davey notched a hat trick, with the other goals coming from Chappell and (a rare one this) Coward.

The next morning Canada rubbed it in by beating the Czechs 7−0, and in the evening Great Britain and USA met in a match crucial to the Olympic and World titles.

The victorious British team (left to right): standing – Jimmy Chappell, Archie Stinchcombe, Alec Archer, Gordon Dailley, Percy Nicklin (coach), Jack Kilpatrick, Carl Erhardt (captain), Johnny Coward, Gerry Davey, P. Vassar Hunter (President BIHA), German journalist; front – Jimmy Borland, Art Child, Jimmy Foster, 'Chirp' Brenchley.

If the Americans won, Britain's only chance would be for the Canadians to inflict a heavy defeat on them so that Britain would win on goal average. If Britain won, it would all be over.

This was the match which the BBC and Bob Bowman broadcast. Both teams were tense and played tight hockey, rarely taking chances. Foster, as usual, was steadiness personified in the British net, and Moon was sound at the other end. Davey nearly scored in the second period, but Moon just managed to deflect the puck. Foster made a lightning lunge to rob Ross close-in and there was some light relief when the Polish referee, trying to get out of the way of a scrimmage, disappeared over the boards and all that could be seen of him were his boots and skates waving in the air. At the end of regular time the score was still 0–0. In overtime Dailley made a beautiful solo rush and hit the post with a terrific shot. Chappell also got through but fell before he could get his shot away.

In the second and third periods of overtime, the Americans seemed fresher than the British and Foster was kept busy, being tested from all angles. Three minutes from the end it looked as if the gallant British defence had been in vain. For once Foster was faked out of position by Gordon Smith, but the American forward, confronted with an open goal, missed.

After the match it was mistakenly announced that Great Britain were the World and Olympic Champions, but then it was realised that if the Americans could beat the Canadians without having a goal scored against them or alternatively could win by more than 5−1, USA would be champions on goal average.

It didn't happen. The States were without their key man and captain, Johnny Garrison, injured against Britain, and were tired after their marathon the previous night. Canada scored early on and preserved their lead to the end.

The final table was thus:

	P	W	L	D	F	A	Pts
Great Britain	3	2	0	1	7	1	5
Canada	3	2	1	0	9	2	4
USA	3	1	1	1	2	1	2
Czechoslovakia	3	0	3	0	0	14	0

Note Each country played only two matches in the final pool, being credited with the result (including goals for and against) of its game with the country that it had met in the semis and which had also reached the final.

Great Britain's triumph was truly a team effort, but it owed much to the sensational goalminding of Jimmy Foster, who racked up four shut-outs in seven games and conceded only three goals altogether. Shots on goal were not kept accurately in those days, but it is said that Foster saved 219 out of 222 shots during the tournament, a fantastic 98.7 per cent of saves to shots.

A great deal of the credit must go to coach Nicklin. His hand first showed in the team selection. He made sure that the styles of the players selected complemented each other and built the team around top goaltending, sound blockers on defence and forwards who skated both ways. No team that Nicklin coached ever lacked backcheckers, and during the three seasons after the Olympics his Harringay Greyhounds and Harringay Racers, especially the Greyhounds, would demonstrate defensive hockey at its best and confound the critics by making it entertaining.

Although at the time of the Olympics squads were smaller (few defencemen today would relish playing unchanged through a game) Nicklin had a tactic which minimised the lack of manpower. He would constantly switch his lines, never leaving anyone on who looked as if they needed a breather. He would also switch lines in order to counter the opposing attacks. If the opposition put out their highest-scoring line, Nicklin would probably put out his best back-checking trio. There was sometimes trouble when the opposing coach realised this, and one night in the English National League 'Nick' and his opposite number were warned by the referees for holding up the game.

Above all, Nicklin had the respect of his players. They knew he had been a top professional himself but, that apart, he was not the sort of man who gave the impression that he could be trifled with. Under that stern exterior, however, there lurked a good sense of humour. Once, with a wink, he told me the secret of being thought wise. 'Let them all argue and you say nothing. See which way the wind is blowing then deliver your considered opinion, making sure that it is in line with the majority. Then everyone will say what a smart guy you are.'

Although Nicklin went on to great success with his Harringay teams and became General Manager of Harringay Arena, he always remembered Garmisch. In 1956 when I wrote an article on the subject for the now defunct London evening newspaper, *The Star*, the first letter I received was from Percy Nicklin, living in Palmers Green, London. 'Thanks, Phil,' he wrote, 'it brought back wonderful memories.'

Credit was also given to Brenchley who scored the winner against Sweden, the first against Japan and the big one, the winner over Canada, amongst his four goals; and to Davey who, despite illness, scored seven goals during the tournament.

The Triple Crown was acclaimed world-wide, apart from official circles in Canada, but then, as Erhardt commented, 'Dealing with a rather difficult type of man, such as the President of the CAHA, was not an easy matter.'

Nicklin had left Canada in a storm over amateurism. He said bluntly that if Canadians were worth anything to a London team then they would be paid. Asked about the 'amateur' Moncton Hawks, he said they were the highest-paid group of hockey players ever to chase an 'amateur' puck. However, when CAHA officials again levelled accusations that hockey in England was a racket and avowed that Canada had been robbed of the Olympic and World Championships by a team of Canadians masquerading as 'Great Britain', they were shot down in flames by the Canadian Press. Ted Reeve, writing in the *Toronto Telegram* commented: 'If Canada cannot beat four or five English-born players who happened to learn their hockey in this country, why we don't deserve the World Championship. So what the whoops is Gilroy [the CAHA President] squawking about?'

There was great enthusiasm for the British victory in Winnipeg where, at that time, two-thirds of the population were British-born or descended from British stock. Clem Shields, of the *Winnipeg Free Press*, declared that he did not like the dictatorial attitude of the CAHA officials 'and if amateur hockey in England is a racket, it has been a racket in Canada for many years.' He also pointed out that although the CAHA had been awkward about the transfer of some sixteen players to the jurisdiction of the British Association, they had not objected to Jimmy Haggarty, of Wembley, whom they wanted to borrow for their own team.

That left only the British captain, Carl Erhardt, with a mild complaint: 'You know, whatever Bob Bowman said on the air, I've never fought on the ice in my life.' Bowman obviously thought the USA v. Great Britain marathon needed a little life injected into it. The free-for-all he described was a mild scrimmage by many standards and resulted in one player being sent off from each team. Erhardt, who according to the commentary was throwing punches as fast as he could, was actually called off the ice by Nicklin, who thought he had been injured in the mêlée. But Bowman's commentary, added to Britain's triumph, was to give British hockey a shot in the arm, the effects of which would last a very long time.

Amidst all the dramas of those days (and nights) in snow-covered Garmisch, the Cockney-born Canadian Gerry Davey could be relied upon for a shaft of humour. In the match against Hungary, Davey, who was being well worked over by one of the opposition, skated up to the American referee Walter Brown (later headman of Boston Bruins) and complained, 'Hey, Walter, watch that big defenceman, eh?' Brown, without moving a muscle of his face, retorted, 'Gee, Gerry, he isn't doing anything to me – you watch him.'

2 FACE-OFF

The surest way to start a fight in Kingston, Ontario, is to suggest that ice hockey, Canada's national sport, originated in Montreal, Quebec.

Montreal certainly has a strong claim. A student at McGill University, W.F. Robertson, visited England and was most impressed with field hockey. On his return to Canada he asked a friend and fellow-student, R.F. Smith, if he could work out some way of playing the game on ice. They used some field hockey rules, some they invented themselves and, for good measure, threw in some rugby rules – hence ice hockey being an 'onside' game. The first game under McGill rules was played in December 1879. The following winter, 1880–81, the first properly organised team came into being – McGill University Hockey Club.

Kingston, largely on the statements of hockey pioneer, Captain James Sutherland, claims that in 1867 the Royal Canadian Rifles, stationed at Tete-du-Pont Barracks, cleared snow from the ice in Kingston Harbour and played a game requiring skates, sticks, goal-posts and a puck, namely hockey on ice.

In further rebuttal of Montreal claims, it is said that in 1870 a British regiment, the 60th Rifles (later the King's Royal Rifle Corps) in which the Duke of Connaught was serving, was taking part in the Red River expedition. According to a Lt. J.W. Marshall, a number of soldiers started a hockey game in the snow but someone then suggested that they put on skates and play on some nearby ice.

Whatever the rights and wrongs of these rival factions, the origin of hockey is, as with most sports, shrouded in the mists of time. Variations of field hockey have been played in different countries for many years and can be traced back at least as far as 500 BC, by Greek reliefs depicting players facing-off with sticks and ball.

The other component of ice hockey, skating, dates back to at least 1134 AD when Norsemen tied bones to their feet, although there is evidence to suggest that others may have used the same methods prior to this date. Skating certainly took place on the frozen Fens of England in medieval times with bone skates, and it also appears from the records that a form of hockey on ice was played which, if so, predates by many years the claims of Kingston and Montreal. Skating is also described in Fitz-Stephen's *Description of London*, published in 1180.

In about 1600 skates with metal blades were introduced to Britain from Holland, and in 1642 the Edinburgh Skating Club, believed to be Britain's oldest skating organisation, was formed. Skating was very popular, especially in the reign of Charles II, and Samuel Pepys and John Evelyn, the diarists, both make reference to it. The first skating publication, *The Art of Skating* by Robert Jones, was published in 1772, and many sketches and paintings during the eighteenth and nineteenth centuries depict people skating on frozen lakes and rivers, often using sticks and a ball or some other object.

In 1876 the first artificial ice rinks were opened in London. In March, John Gamgee opened The Glaciarium in Kings Road, Chelsea, followed by another under the same name at the Charing Cross end of Northumberland Avenue where a swimming-pool was frozen. The rink manager and skating instructor was an American, Robert G. Austin.

Across the Atlantic, in 1885 a member of the original McGill Ice Hockey Club, A.P. Low, introduced the sport to Ottawa, and in 1888 the Ottawa Rebels came into being. Montreal Victorias and Quebec Crystals were other early clubs.

The Rebels were formed by The Hon. Arthur Stanley, son of Lord Stanley of Preston, then Governor-General of Canada, and two years later he also formed the Ontario Hockey Association. In 1893 he and his hockey-playing brothers persuaded their father to present the Stanley Cup which became emblematic of the world professional ice hockey championship and was contested by such great clubs as Montreal Canadiens, Detroit Red Wings, Toronto Maple Leafs, New York Rangers, Boston Bruins, Chicago Black Hawks and others. In the same year, A.C.A. Wade, one of the first ice hockey writers, recalls playing ice hockey at Gravenhurst in Bedfordshire.

On their return to England the Stanley sons continued to encourage the spread of ice hockey. During the hard winter of 1895 the lake at Buckingham Palace was frozen over, and a Palace team which included the Prince of Wales (later King Edward VII), the Duke of York (King George V), Lord Mildmay, Sir Francis Astley-Corbett, Sir William Bromley Davenport and Mr Ronald Moncrieff, played the Stanley team, led by Lord Stanley (afterwards the Earl of Derby) and including four more Stanley brothers plus Lord Annally. The Palace, not surprisingly in view of the Stanleys' experience, were well-beaten.

Pedants might argue as to whether or not it was truly ice hockey, both sides using bandy sticks, but in the formative years of the game the dividing line between hockey, bandy and shinty

The Old Aquarium at Westminster had a non-ice surface long before the plastic portable skating surfaces of the 1970s and 1980s. Photo shows modern plastic surface installed in a club at Cardiff.

was always a fine one.

The Duke of Connaught had already been introduced to the game during his service in Canada and this match at Buckingham Palace marked the beginning of a Royal interest in the sport which would survive through to Queen Elizabeth II, Prince Philip and their sons.

In 1896 Londoners saw posters everywhere advertising 'real ice skating at the Niagara Hall, near St James's Park Station, Westminster.' The Niagara, Henglers and Princes were all to become popular, and for a period all three were running simultaneously. There was also a rink at the Old Aquarium, Westminster, which had a slippery surface but was *not* ice. So the plastic ice rinks which were to appear after the Second World War were not such an innovation as many people thought.

The Stanley family continued their missionary work at the new rink, and in the 1896—7 season Lord Stanley and five of his brothers played the Niagara team and beat them very easily. Victor Stanley, who did not play in the Palace match, replaced Lord Annally to make the Stanley team one hundred per cent family. Two of the Stanley brothers, A.F. and F.W., also played for an Old Wellingtonians team which lost 2—0 to Niagara on 1 January 1899.

The Stanleys were a truly remarkable family. All the brothers were much decorated in later life, one became an Admiral, another a General and at least two more reached high military rank. It was a great pity that Arthur, the best puck-chaser of them all and the founder of Ottawa Rebels, did not play in

England, having to give up the sport after an attack of rheumatic fever. Instead, he turned his attention to another activity then in its formative years, motoring, and as Sir Arthur Stanley, GCVO, GBE, CB, he was Chairman of the Royal Automobile Club from 1905 to 1907 and again from 1912 to 1936.

Thus it can be seen that the introduction of hockey was a rather piecemeal affair. Arguments still rage. Some historians believe that bandy on the Fens was the real origin; others that the English garrison which introduced the idea at Halifax, Nova Scotia, in 1870 were the true progenitors of the sport.

The first official ice hockey match outside Canada is said to have been Cambridge University v. Oxford University at St Moritz in 1885, Oxford winning 6−0. The centenary of this was marked in 1985 by the presentation of plaques to the current Oxford and Cambridge teams by the President of the British Ice Hockey Association, Fred Meredith.

What was played in that match was probably not ice hockey as we know it. Certainly bandy and/or ice hockey was popular in St Moritz and Davos and in Berlin in the 1890s. What does seem to be unquestioned is that the students of McGill were responsible for drawing up the rules on which ice hockey is still based today, although naturally there have been many alterations over the years. They also staged the first match under these rules and they formed the first club specifically to play matches under the same rules.

Indeed, Kingston's claim to be first is somewhat weakened by other evidence from the selfsame Captain Sutherland. In 1886 a match was recorded at Kingston between Queen's University and the Royal Military College. But, according to Captain Sutherland, hockey sticks had to be borrowed – *from Montreal*. Kingston, however, not to be beaten, opened the International Hockey Hall of Fame and Museum to yells of outrage from Montreal. Toronto also now has a Hall of Fame.

One can't help feeling that Kingston has taken the whole matter much too seriously. Their Hall of Fame is advertised as 'The world's original hockey shrine'. Sport is a religion to some people, but shrine seems to be carrying it a little too far.

The arguments as to who invented ice hockey are likely to continue for many years. And why not? What better way of spending a long winter evening when there isn't a match than by chewing the fat over a libation or two? To start the argument off again, my view is that the British invented the game and played it on the Fens in the Middle Ages. The British re-invented it in 1867 and 1870 when British soldiers played in Canada, and again in 1879 when the 'McGills' adapted British field hockey and its rules. Score: Great Britain 3, The Rest 0.

3 OVER THE BLUE-LINE

Wagers, fist-fights, community warfare and editorial sniping may accompany the discussion on who 'invented' ice hockey, but there is little doubt that the sport's 'Founding Father' in the United Kingdom was a great English gentleman, Major B.M. 'Peter' Patton. It was he who approached Admiral Maxe, founder of Princes' Skating Club and asked that awe-inspiring personage for permission to form an ice hockey club at the rink. Permission was given and the first match took place in February 1897. Patton was then 21 and he did not retire as a player until 1931 when he was 55 years of age. During those 34 years he filled every position at one time or another – forward, defence and goal. The team he founded, often playing as England, upheld the country's prestige on the Continent in fine style. Princes played in an international bandy tournament at Davos in 1904 and won, and in the same year represented England at Lyons where they beat France.

In 1908 England (again represented by Princes) won the first indoor International Ice Hockey Tournament in Berlin where they defeated Germany and France in hard-fought games. Later in the same season of 1908–09, playing as Princes, they won the Grindelwald Cup for the third time, and playing as England they won the International Ice Hockey Championship at Chamonix.

The first European Championship was held at Les Avants, Switzerland, in 1910, and 'Peter' Patton, by now a veteran of 34, captained the England team. Five teams took part: England, Germany, Belgium, Switzerland and Oxford Canadians, but the latter's results did not, of course, count for the Championship. Oxford were included in the tournament to show the Swiss public how the Canadians played.

In the competition proper, England beat Switzerland and Germany and drew with Belgium and as the only unbeaten team became the first official European Champions. In goal England had air pioneer Tommy Sopwith, whose fighter aircraft were to play a prominent role in the First World War; on defence were Patton and B.C. Cox (in those days, as in field hockey and soccer, they called them backs) and the forwards were H.H. Duden, R.N. Le Cron and J. Cox. It was a fine performance by the England team since two of their best players, A.N. Macklin and R.D. Nolan, were injured and unable to play, while Duden played with a broken bone in his shoulder strapped up.

England climaxed a great season by crushing Scotland 11–1 at Princes in the first match ever played between the two countries.

Patton last played on defence in 1923 when England won the Kulm International Challenge Cup at St Moritz for the second time. After that he played in goal for several years, and on more than one occasion was the only true Englishman in the England team against Canada. He was one of two goaltenders in 1927 when Montreal Victorias, the first Canadian team to visit Britain, won 14–1 or 15–1 according to which newspaper you read. What is certain is that Patton played in the third period and conceded only two goals. His last match of international stature was in 1931 when he was nearly 56. He played in goal for London against Paris in the second match to be staged at the Velodrome d'hiver.

He founded the British Ice Hockey Association in 1913 and revived it, after it had been disbanded during the war, in 1923. He held the office of President until 1934 when he was succeeded by Philip Vassar Hunter.

Ice hockey developed steadily during Patton's prime playing years. On 4 January 1899 Brighton defeated Princes 4–2, the first stirrings of what was eventually to become a great hockey town in Sussex. Princes could, perhaps, be forgiven for succumbing to the Brightonians. It must have been disconcerting to say the least to find that the home rink was completely circular.

Oxford played Cambridge in 1900. Oxford were captained by B.T.J. Bosanquet, the England cricketer credited with inventing the slow ball known today as the 'wrong 'un', otherwise the 'googly' or the 'bosy', after its inventor. Bosanquet's son, Reggie, became well known as a television news-reader and presenter.

The 1902–03 season saw competition intensifying, with Princes facing challenges from teams from Henglers Circus Ice Rink, also known as the National Ice Palace, and the newly-formed London Canadians. Spice was added to the season when the touring Canadian Rugby side doffed their football kit and put on skates for an exhibition match against their London compatriots. The Rugby players won 5–3. London Canadians had some consolation when they defeated Princes in the final of the Princes Challenge Trophy after extra time.

The following season (1903–04) saw the formation of the first English Ice Hockey League with five teams taking part: Princes; two teams from Henglers, Argyll and the Amateur Skating Club; London Canadians; and Cambridge. Canadians won the Championship with fourteen points, two more than the runners-up, Princes. Internationally, however, Princes were still doing well with three wins over Lyons and another against Paris in Paris.

Royal patronage of the sport continued; King Edward VII and Queen Alexandra attended a match between London and an International Select at Henglers on 4 February 1904. The Internationals won a close game. The Royal party included the King and Queen of Norway, accompanied by Prince Christian; the Prince and Princess of Wales (later King George V and Queen Mary); Princess Victoria; and the Duke of Connaught. Both King Edward and his son, George, had played ice hockey themselves, and it is probable that the Duke of Connaught had done so during his service in Canada.

There was something of a set-back the following winter when London Canadians disbanded after beating Princes early in the season, but the Patton outfit continued their winning ways both on the Continent and at home.

Oxford Canadians were formed in 1905–06 and did much to fill the gap left by London Canadians. Lyons visited Princes and the home side had a comfortable 9–1 victory. The new team brought great interest into the game and 1906–07 saw a series of matches between them and Princes, most of which were won by the older-established team. But the Cup match in March went to the Canadians 8–4.

Prior to this Princes had won the Grindelwald Cup in January and then went on to win the Lyon Challenge Trophy for the third successive time, beating Sporting Club de Lyons home and away. They also defeated the Club des Patineurs of Brussels home and away. In the return match in London, Princes iced a reserve squad as the first team had played Oxford Canadians earlier in the evening. Princes won 17–1, and of those seventeen goals, C.M.G. Howell scored fifteen, a world record. Rather surprisingly, in the years he played for Cambridge University, Howell had been a defenceman.

Princes continued to be the top British team through 1907–08, when, apart from winning the Grindelwald Challenge Cup again, they won most of their matches at home and abroad, and the following seasons saw their triumphs in Berlin and in the European Championship.

1910 was an important year for British ice hockey. Apart from England winning the European Championship, it was also the year when the Manchester Ice Palace opened its doors – a rink which was to play a vital role in the sport right through to the Second World War. Hockey was played from the start, and by 1913 the Ice Palace was using in its advertising the slogan *the*

Paris, where 'Peter' Patton played his last international match at the age of 55. The team practising are Toronto Dukes, visitors to Britain in the early 1930s. The tall man watching the scrimmage is coach 'Moose' Ecclestone.

fastest game on earth, the first-known use of the phrase in Britain.

Manchester started with a pretty strong team, and when Princes visited the rink in 1910–11 the London squad were beaten 5–3. In some ways it was the beginning of the end of their supremacy. They lost to Scotland 8–3, although in fairness the then Crossmyloof rink, which had a bandstand on pillars in the centre of the ice pad, must have been disconcerting to visiting firemen. A tricky centreman could have had a very interesting time using the bandstand pillars as supporting body-checkers.

Christmas seemed to put new heart into the Londoners. They defeated the first German side to visit Great Britain 8–3, and then went to Les Avants where they beat Switzerland and Belgium but lost to Germany and Oxford Canadians. At

Chamonix just afterwards they lost all three matches played, although they were handicapped by injuries. Defeated in Paris at the start of the following season, Princes gained a sort of second-hand glory when four of their players – Batting (goal), Le Cron, Sullivan and Patton – helped Les Avants to win the Swiss Championship.

After Princes had won yet another international tournament at Les Avants early in 1913, 'Peter' Patton, Lord Carberry and Patton's team-mate on the European Championship team H.H. Duden, got together with The Hon. F.N. Curzon, of St Moritz Bandy Club, and formed a new organisation, the St Moritz Bandy and Ice Hockey Club. The significance of this is emphasised by Patton's own comment: 'This is how ice hockey came to be introduced into the Engadine and at St Moritz, which, like Davos, had hitherto been a stronghold of bandy.' In the light of this it seems most unlikely that the game Oxford and Cambridge played at St Moritz in 1885 was actually ice hockey; it was almost certainly bandy. Celebrating the occasion, Patton then organised an International Ice Hockey Tournament in which five countries took part. Germany beat England 5–4 in the decisive game, England having to be content with second place.

By this time the war clouds were gathering over Europe, and the 1913–14 season was to be the last for a long time. Yet it was also to mark a milestone in the game. The British Ice Hockey Association was formed with Patton as President and T.G. Cannon as Hon. Secretary and Treasurer. The founder member clubs were Princes, Oxford Canadians, Cambridge, Manchester and Royal Engineers (Chatham).

Princes represented England in an International Tournament at Les Avants and the Championship of the International Ice Hockey League at Chamonix and, being able to ice a strong team for both tournaments, emerged victorious.

The International League (formed in 1908) was at least a major honour for Britain's puck-chasers to recall in the long bleak years which lay ahead. Sadly, many of these pioneers of the sport, both British and Canadian, would never return to play again. The legacy they left behind was the foundation-stone of a magnificent sport which, when peace came, would gradually develop into one where, instead of a few well-to-do young men learning the game in Switzerland, young players would come up from the mines of Fifeshire, from the teeming streets of Glasgow and London and from the industrial towns and villages of the North; a game which instead of being watched by a handful of friends of the players would attract crowds of 10,000 to magnificent stadiums, purpose-built for the sport.

All that lay a long way ahead as the British Expeditionary Force embarked for Flanders.

4 IN THE PENALTY-BOX

The aftermath of one of the bloodiest slaughters in the history of the world was hardly a fruitful time for a sport not yet established nationally to grow and flourish. With many a wage-earner dead, others unemployed, officers misguidedly taking up chicken farms and smallholdings and manufacturers building lightweight cyclecars to meet the demands of a straitened economy, ice hockey was back at square one.

Patton, enthusiasm undiminished, started to build up the sport once more, but was greatly handicapped by the shortage of rinks in the United Kingdom willing and able to stage ice hockey matches. Once again it was a question of British players going to Switzerland if they wanted a game. Oxford v. Cambridge was revived at Murren in 1920, and Patton afterwards recruited players from both teams, added the English international G.E. Clarkson, and went on to win the Bouvier Cup in St Moritz.

This was to be the pattern of the next two or three seasons. A rather farcical European Championship had been held in Stockholm in 1921, the home country winning a *two* nation contest and Great Britain being absent. Against such a background it took a group of incurable optimists to stage the Championships again the following winter, but this is just what the St Moritz Ice Hockey Club, some Swiss officials and Patton did, running the Championships in conjunction with an international tournament. An 'English' team comprising Patton in goal and five of the Oxford University team carried all before them and were declared winners of the international tournament and the Kulm Cup, but Czechoslovakia won the European title as the five Oxford players were Canadians.

Another 'English' team retained the Kulm Cup by defeating Davos the following season. This time Patton recruited Canadian officers from a British Army team which had played several matches in St Moritz.

In 1923 Manchester Ice Palace was the only rink staging ice hockey in England and the hockey was often primitive by modern standards. One player of the time said that the usual equipment comprised a pair of soccer shinguards, a pair of stout gloves and liberal coatings of embrocation. Despite this the British Ice Hockey Association was revived, with Patton and Cannon occupying their original offices of President and Secretary and Treasurer respectively.

Brothers Bert and George Shaw who arrived in England 'on spec' in the early 1930s. Bert (above) joined Warwickshire (later Birmingham Maple Leafs) and then went to Manchester before coaching on the Continent. George (right) went to Streatham, played on their Championship team and became one of the outstanding players in the English National League.

Manchester continued to play an important role in British hockey through the 1920s and 1930s. The 1926 BIHA Handbook reports the Lancashire club playing matches against Princes, Oxford and Cambridge Universities and – a rare name on the Great Ice Way – Leeds University. P.L. Rothband, Millington and Joe Cock were amongst the earlier top players, Cock continuing on into the veteran stage. The team had the support of the rink directors, one of whom, Leslie Hood, took an active role. Unfortunately, he broke his nose in his very first game.

Johnson and Melland, both mentioned elsewhere, were probably Manchester's best home-grown players over the years, but at different times the team also had some useful Canadians including Bert Shaw, brother of Streatham's George, 'Chuck' Stapleford, brother of another Streatham luminary, 'Red', and the ever-popular Les Tapp.

The Winter Olympics were to be held in Chamonix in 1924. (Olympic ice hockey had been held for the first time at Antwerp in 1920 when Canada, represented by Winnipeg Falcons, were the winners. Britain had been unable to raise a team.) Now a request was made by the British Olympic Association that a team should be sent to Chamonix; Manchester put the Ice Palace at the services of the selectors and a trial match was played, British Army v. The Rest, the latter winning a close match 4–3.

Thus Britain's first Olympic team was chosen and it comprised two Englishmen and nine Canadians qualified by residence. The player-coach was the selfsame Clarkson already mentioned, who had played for Toronto University in 1912 but had been resident in Britain since. Every effort was made to ensure a good performance, and the team went to Switzerland for two weeks training prior to the Games.

Eight teams played at Chamonix, and Toronto Granites, who represented Canada, were out on their own. They achieved some fantastic scores: 33–0 against Switzerland, 30–0 against Czechoslovakia and 22–0 against Sweden, in Pool A; and then 19–2 against Great Britain and 6–1 against the USA in the final round, despite the Americans including two hockey 'greats' Bobby Abel and Herb Drury. Drury was rated the man of the tournament and the fastest ever seen in Europe up to that point.

Great Britain finished third to Canada and USA, thus helping this country to be third in the overall placings of the twelve competing nations despite the fact that Britain did not take part in the ski events. This historic British squad was: B.M. Patton, G.E. Clarkson, B.N. Sexton, L.H. Carr Harris, E.D. Carruthers, G.C. Carruthers, MC, C. Ross Cuthbert, MC, H.D. Jukes, E.B. Pitblado, C.B. Boulden and W.H. Anderson.

Unfortunately, the rule was not then in force that the highest-placed European team in the Olympic and World Championships automatically became European Champions. When the European Championships were held later in the season, Britain could not gather a team together.

Nevertheless, Olympic bronze did help to increase interest at home, and the following season, Blane Sexton, a member of the Olympic team, founded the London Lions, who were to become a famous name. They still, however, had to play most of their matches in Switzerland, which they did very successfully in 1924–25 and 1925–26. Their formation enabled Britain to enter the European Championships (held at Davos) once again and finish fourth. Britain lost 4–3 in overtime to the eventual winners, Switzerland, and the lack of good reserves (as substitutes were then known) was a big factor. In those days teams were allowed only two reserves plus a spare goalminder, so unless the reserves were really good players the starting six not surprisingly tired in overtime.

In 1926 ice hockey's long sojourn in the sin-bin showed signs of ending. The Ice Club at Millbank, Westminster, London, was opened. Carl Erhardt observed, rather sadly, that it was 'wide open for fancy skaters with a good knowledge of skating and prepared to pay the rather heavy subscription, but only just open for ice hockey players who were merely tolerated, and although they also had to pay a substantial subscription for being permitted to practise from 9 p.m. to 11 p.m. on Monday nights were really looked upon as a nuisance.' Despite this, it marked the beginning of the game's new growth. The Duke of York (later King George VI) was one of those who played there.

International matches were staged at the Ice Club. The first Canadian team to visit England, Montreal Victorias, defeated England 14–1 (or 15–1, as discussed earlier). The home team was composed of resident Canadians with the exception of Patton, who played the third period in goal and conceded only two scores. Sexton, the captain, scored England's only goal, also in the third period. Later in the season, England played Belgium at the Ice Club and won 3–1.

Princes Club was re-formed, and soon rinks were to be opened at Richmond, Hammersmith, Bayswater, Golders Green, Hove, Park Lane, Oxford, Birmingham and Liverpool. Alas, most of the builders made a major mistake which unfortunately was to be repeated in the ice rink boom of the 1980s – they did not provide sufficient spectator accommodation to make it a viable proposition to promote hockey. As a result, some of the rinks opened in high expectations were soon converted to cinemas or dance-halls.

However, for the moment most of the activity took place at the Ice Club, 'nuisance' or not, although in January 1928 the rink was flooded and out of action. Great Britain entered the Winter Olympics and after winning their pool, lost to Switzerland, Sweden and Canada in the final and had to be content with fourth place. Although beaten 14−0 by Canada, the British team fought hard and attacked constantly, but Sullivan was brilliant in the Canadian goal. So the lop-sided score was a little misleading.

The British team was Speechley (Cambridge) and Rogers (Zuos College) in goal; Wylde (Cambridge), Hurst Brown (London Canadians) and Vic Tait (United Services) on defence; Ross Cuthbert, S.R. and C.G. Carruthers and Greenwood (all United Services), Neville Melland (Manchester) and Fawcett (Rosey College), forwards. Melland would be durable enough still to be a contender for the 1936 Olympic team when he was playing with Richmond Hawks.

The Canadian Olympic team later visited England and beat the home country 11−4 at the Ice Club, but the visiting Belgian team was again defeated.

Another step forward came the following season with the opening of the Richmond rink and the first of many matches there, continuing − with interruptions − to the present day. Blane Sexton's team played the Services there and drew 4−4.

Internationally, there was much activity at club level. St Moritz visited London for the first time and drew with a BIHA Select at the Ice Club; a BIHA team visited St Moritz, Prague, Vienna and Budapest and then German and Swedish teams visited Britain. The Swedes, playing here for the first time, caused some concern with their 'rough play' at Richmond.

From 1928 to 1933 the English Club Championship was shared equally between United Services, London Lions and Oxford, each with two wins apiece. However, this was the swan-song of the gifted amateur, Canadian or English, because the day of the specially-imported player was nigh.

Much more ice hockey was being played during this period as Golders Green, Hammersmith, Hove and the Park Lane Ice Club came into the picture, and in Scotland the big Glasgow rink was reopened and the Scottish Ice Hockey Association formed, of which more anon. Any Canadian living or working in London who had ever worn a pair of skates was pressed into service, there not being enough home-grown talent to go round. One high-scoring forward, N.S. Grace, was so keen on the game that he would turn up wherever a match was scheduled and volunteer if a team was short-handed, which they frequently were in those days.

The newspapers were now giving a fair bit of coverage to the sport, largely due to pioneer hockey reporters like A.C.A. Wade, Jack Dixon, Eric Green and 'Potty' Pottinger, so that 'N.S. Grace' would be seen variously as playing for Princes,

United Services, London Lions, Grosvenor House and a few other teams for good measure.

The first Japanese team to visit Britain was here in the 1929–30 season, playing matches at Hammersmith and the Ice Club and losing both, 7–3 to England and 4–3 to Cambridge. They were later to be amongst Britain's opponents in the 1936 Olympics. With more rinks active there was greater public interest, heightened by the visit of Canada, who played at Hove and Golders Green, and also of St Moritz and the French national team.

Young talent was given more encouragement than hitherto, and Princes second team won the Hunter Cup, emblematic of the Junior League Championship. The trophy had been donated by Philip Vassar Hunter, a member of the winning team who was later to become President of the British Ice Hockey Association. In view of the arguments over the origins of ice hockey, it is interesting to note that Vassar Hunter, born in Norfolk, learned to play the game on the frozen Fens, *but* it was the version known as bandy.

Officials today who worry about the season being too long should take heed that this season did not end until 17 May when London Lions beat Glasgow 2–1 for the Patton Cup.

The following season also went on into May, the last match of the campaign being between London Lions and Queen's at the Bayswater rink, of which Carl Erhardt said: 'The long and narrow character of the ice surface never permitted a game to develop attractively.'

Many years later, I recall Jo Bonnier, the ill-fated Swedish Grand Prix driver, demonstrating the value of studded tyres on ice at Queen's Club. It struck me very forcibly that this rink could so easily have been a hotbed of hockey, situated as it is in such a well-populated area of the West End of London and accessible from all parts by the Underground system with a station almost adjacent. Queen's, over the years, has produced many talented ice skaters and that, alas, must remain its major claim to fame.

Back in 1930–31 the Germans played a four-game series against England which ended with two drawn games and one win apiece. In another match the visitors defeated Oxford 2–1.

The British team played in Switzerland before going on to Poland and the World and European Championships, the famous occasion where Field Marshal Pilsudski, the President of Poland, fell full-length on the ice as he was about to be introduced. The British team lost to Austria after 30 minutes overtime, and the Austrians went on to win the European title.

Gerry Davey

B. Shaw

Harvey "Red" Stapleford

They were captained by 'Dickie' von Trauttenberg, who was also captain of that year's Cambridge team and went on to become a regular defenceman with Streatham. The Canadians won the World title and took in Great Britain on their way home.

The 1931–32 season was a landmark in the story of British ice hockey, with overseas visitors including Ottawa, Boston, Zurich, Austria and a German team, and, probably of greater importance to the development of the game in the United Kingdom, a series of matches in London against the Scottish League. The Boston team was brought over by Walter Brown, who was to bring over many more US teams and eventually become boss of the professional Boston Bruins, but who was always to remain a great and staunch friend of British ice hockey.

Britain found a new international star in 1931, teenage Gerry Davey, seen above with two Streatham team-mates in 1936, George Shaw and Harvey 'Red' Stapleford. They made a great combination with Shaw at centre, Davey on right-wing and Stapleford on left.

The Varsity match was played in England for the first time since 1901. Great Britain was seventh out of nine in the European Championships, won by Sweden, but unearthed a teenage star, Gerry Davey, who was to have a long and illustrious career in both the English and Scottish Leagues. Oxford won the League for the first time and emphasised their right to the title by beating The Rest 2–1.

A new rink was opened in Paris and the first match there featured London's Grosvenor House Canadians. The Canadians, formed in December 1929, were the advance guard of a new deal in the game. The management looked around for the best players, most of them Canadians, and from there it was a short step to importing stars from Canada. The man behind Grosvenor House was a Canadian in business in London, F.L. 'Freddie' Summerhayes, who later was to be the instigator of hockey at Earls Court. He first went to Golders Green with his ideas, and when they turned him down he went to Grosvenor House. There is a good case for regarding him as the originator of the modern British game.

The Park Lane rink was on the small side for hockey, although 1,500 spectators could squeeze in at a pinch – circumstances which led to it being very hot and stuffy, according to Carl Erhardt. It was in just such an atmosphere that Grosvenor House, regarded as interlopers, met London Lions, who had been dominant for some time, in a challenge match and it led to one of the first of ice hockey's big fights. Tempers were frayed, there were two or three pushing and shoving matches and the spectators joined in, some of them picking up sticks and throwing them on to the ice. 'But,' said A.C.A. Wade, 'it was a trifling affair compared with many in later years.'

A pillar of the Grosvenor House team was Ottawa-born George Strubbe whose active hockey days had ended, or so he thought, with the First World War. He came to London in 1923 and in 1927 heard that ice hockey was being played at the London Ice Club. He went along to watch, met British international Vic Tait and was persuaded to join London Lions. After twelve years on the sidelines his first few matches were painful experiences, but he soon got into the swing of things and became a prominent figure in the sport. He left London Lions for Hammersmith, where he formed the Hammersmith ice hockey club together with Scot Jimmy Brown, the first British indoor speed skating champion over a mile, and Dr Thorold McDiarmid Kellough.

Long after British hockey became a commercial spectator sport, 'Doc' was still running a happy-go-lucky vagabond

A rare photo of the English women's team practising at Queens, Bayswater, in 1934 for an international match against France. Women began playing in Britain before 1928 and the first clubs were Manchester Women, Manchester Merlins, London Lambs, Queens Ladies and Brighton & Hove. The sport was so little known that the original caption writer for this picture referred to 'the ball'.

Queens team. Others who played at the London Ice Club included Canadian Brigadier-General A.C. Critchley (later to build a Harringay Arena modelled on the lines of Toronto's Maple Leaf Gardens) and pioneer racing driver, wartime flying ace and top bob-sledder of Cresta Run fame, Lord Brabazon of Tara.

Claude Langdon, who ran Hammersmith, realised that it was far from ideal for ice hockey and moved the refrigeration machinery down the road to Richmond Rink which had been closed for two years, no less than three companies going bankrupt during its short lifetime. It was the saving of Richmond which still flourishes today, while Hammersmith became the most famous Palais de Danse in Britain.

Langdon later joined the Brighton board and eventually became the top man at Empress Hall. It was he who invited Wembley's Arthur Elvin to see his first ice hockey match which led to the building of the Empire Pool & Sports Arena. Meanwhile, Strubbe and some friends, backed by Summerhayes, operated two teams at Grosvenor House and these were eventually to provide the nucleus of Wembley Canadians. The association between Summerhayes, Langdon and Strubbe lasted a long time, George managing the Earls Court and Brighton teams.

1932 also saw another milestone. On 18 January England played Ottawa at Grosvenor House, the first ice hockey match to be broadcast in Britain. Alas for the listeners, England were trounced 7—0.

Oxford were League champions for the second successive season in 1932–33, but the home competition was rather overshadowed by international activity. A BIHA team visited France and Switzerland, and a positive deluge of overseas teams visited Britain. Purley and Southampton were amongst the rinks staging international matches. Racing Club de Paris, Germany, Edmonton Superiors, Toronto, Boston Rangers – all played a number of matches against both club and representative sides, and such was the interest that there were even two matches between Toronto and Boston.

In a drawn game between Boston Rangers and Streatham on 27 March two referees officiated for the first time in Britain.

For most followers of the sport the highlight of the season came on 23 January when England met Edmonton Eskimos at Hammersmith. The Canadians equalised just before the final whistle to rob England of what would have been a famous victory.

The Hammersmith rink must have had special 'vibes' for the England team. Two years earlier they had come close to beating Canada, losing 3–2 after taking a 2–1 lead. Carr Harris and Jimmy Brown (assisted by the aforementioned N.S. Grace) scored the home goals, but the closeness of the struggle owed a lot to England's goalminder, Vic Gardner, who played a 'blinder'. Gardner, who earned 124 international caps, was one of the best English goalies of all time and captained the team in the 1932 European Championships. Many years later I was introduced to him by another old player, and Vic, a charming man, told me much about the art of goaltending. A very modest man, he was reluctant to claim too much credit for shut-outs, of which he had many to his name, pointing out one match in Austria which the England team won 16–0 and in which he didn't have a shot to save. He also registered a shut-out against the Japanese team when they visited England in 1930.

Another great goalie and shut-out king around this time was Oxford's Herbie Little, who also played for England. Neither Gardner or Little though, could yet match as characters another goalminder, Jimmy Justice, later to become a famous film actor and star of the *Doctor In The House* series as James Robertson Justice.

Forced to retire from goalminding after a skiing injury, Justice became a BIHA official and referee. The highlight of his career as a referee came in a match at Golders Green between England and Austria. Justice ordered off the Austrian netman, who took one look at the towering giant and went, but his team-mates felt there was safety in numbers and they all skated off in protest. Fortunately the Austrian Ambassador was present and he persuaded his countrymen to resume the game.

1933 was a noteworthy year for another reason. An event occurred off the ice, involving a man who not only couldn't play ice hockey, he couldn't even skate. J.F. 'Bunny' Ahearne, an extrovert Irishman who, as a travel agent, had been handling arrangements for touring teams was appointed Secretary of the British Ice Hockey Association. He was to become not only the major figure in the British game, but a dominant influence in the sport both in Europe and world-wide.

At the same time 'Peter' Patton was succeeded as BIHA President by Philip Vassar Hunter. It marked the end of an era for many reasons, not least that Grosvenor House and Queens had been recruiting good quality players and were dominating competitive hockey. Defending champions Oxford declared that they had never played against so many top-class Canadians as appeared in the Grosvenor House and Queens colours. Under the circumstances they were pleased to finish a gallant third in the League.

Crowd-pleaser at Queens was tricky little French-Canadian Frankie Leblanc, a high-scoring centre with a short stick, who was later to join Strubbe with Wembley Canadians. Queens beat Français Volants on home ice and also had a highly successful Continental tour. Ottawa Shamrocks, Boston Rangers, Austria and France all visited England in addition to the Volants, but there was still a great deal of interest in the home competitions. The Press were giving a little more coverage to the sport and more spectators were attending.

It was worth the admittance charge to see a man like Leblanc, a dipsy-doodle type of player who would show the puck to a defender and then dance away, ice hockey's version of football's Stanley Matthews. In the modern game, with the accent on speed, slap-shots and mauling, clever players of Leblanc's style are rarely seen. Born in Montreal, the centreman had an impeccable hockey pedigree before joining Queens, his previous clubs being Montreal Royals and Moncton Hawks.

A fine player of different style, big, robust George Shaw, from Stratford, Ontario, arrived in England around this time and joined Streatham where he was to become a key figure in the team. A flier during the war, he played a lot of Services hockey before retiring.

Grosvenor House's all-round strength gave them the title and the season ended with a 7–7 tie against The Rest.

Ice hockey must be in the blood. Shaw, in retirement, still remembers 'the sportsmanship of English fans and the fellowship of the other players'. Talking of 'in the blood', John Carr Harris, born in London 26 July 1920 to one of England's Army internationals, played professional hockey in the 1940s with Washington, of the American Hockey League. The game certainly stays in the family once the bug has bitten!

5 OFF THE BENCH

The year 1936 was a significant one in Scottish ice hockey. The five-team League, in reality a Glasgow City League, attracted packed houses at many of the matches and the seasonal attendance was the highest yet recorded. Amid all the euphoria, the Scottish international team, with a record of four losses to the 'auld enemy', drew 1–1 with England at Crossmyloof before more than 3,000 excited fans. Both sides included British-born Canadians from the English National League and the public appetite was whetted by fast, good quality, end-to-end hockey.

Scotland had Olympic hero Jimmy Foster in goal; 'Scotty' McAlpine, Earls Court Rangers' husky captain, and his rugged team-mate Paul MacPhail on defence; and 'Scotty' Cameron, of Kensington Corinthians, amongst the forwards. The rest of the team was made up of Glasgow players: John and Billy Fullerton, Jim Kenny and Ronald MacDonald (all of Mohawks); Johnny Kelly (Mustangs) and Sid Montford (Kelvingrove).

England were represented by Art Child (Wembley Lions) in goal; Carl Erhardt and Ernie Ramus (Streatham) on defence; Alec Archer, Jack Kilpatrick (Wembley Lions), 'Chirp' Brenchley, Johnny Coward (Richmond Hawks), Jimmy Shannon and Ralph Groome (Kensington Corinthians) as forwards.

Brenchley scored for England two minutes after the start on a pass from Archer, but after that Foster was in Olympic form and handled everything that Coward, Archer and Kilpatrick fired at him. There were near misses at both ends, the game being played at a very fast pace. The native Scots played well. MacDonald did well when given his chance on defence alongside McAlpine, the Earls Court giant pleasing the crowd with his solo rushes, and Billy Fullerton was as fast as any player on the ice. In fact, late in the season though it was, Earls Court were so impressed with Billy Fullerton that he was invited to London for a try-out. He was offered terms but returned home to 'think it over'.

It looked as if Scotland would have to settle for a narrow defeat, beaten but not disgraced. Erhardt and Ramus were blocking well, and Child saved everything coming his way. Then, in the dying minutes, Cameron latched on to the puck by his own net and stick-handled his way through the opposition to fire a low hard shot at the English goalie. Child padded it away, but Cameron was on hand for the rebound and whipped it smartly into the net.

For a hard core of Scottish enthusiasts that match and its outcome was some justification for years of hard work.

In the years since the First World War Scottish ice hockey players, apart from occasional outdoor matches, had largely been in the position of warming the bench and watching the game develop in England, primarily because of the absence of indoor rinks in Scotland. Then, in 1928, the Scottish Ice Rink Company was formed with the intention of building a new rink on the site of the old Crossmyloof rink in Glasgow, which had closed down in 1918. That was the rink where a few early matches had been played, and where the Princes team had been somewhat disconcerted to find that they had to stick-handle round a bandstand on stilts in the middle of the ice surface.

The people behind the project were more interested in curling and figure skating than ice hockey, and when enthusiasts who had been playing outdoor matches at Bearsden and Loch Ardinning approached the management they were given little encouragement. Fortunately, however, two of the directors took a different view, and thus in 1929 the Scottish Ice Hockey Association was formed and matches took place at the new rink.

The two directors who listened sympathetically were Frank Stuart, chairman of the rink company who became President of the SIHA, and Andrew Mitchell, who became Vice-President. The four players who made the initial approaches were two Canadians, Stewie Lindsay and Hugh Reid, and two natives, J.R. Gilmour and G.C. Scott, the latter a noted rugby player. Gilmour subsequently became Secretary of the SIHA and captained the Scottish team in 1932 and again in 1933. Scots should mark their names with pride.

Founder member clubs were Glasgow Canadians, Bearsden, Bridge of Weir, Doonside, Achtungs, Queens, Dennistoun, Kelvingrove, Glasgow Skating Club and Scottish Corinthians. The latter two clubs included some of the players who had appeared in pre First World War fixtures, amongst them J.B. Wharrie, the Scottish goalie in 1910.

Serious hockey started in 1929–30 with most of the founder clubs competing, apart from Canadians and Corinthians whose places were taken by Mohawks and Glasgow University. Each team played four matches and according to their results were placed in either the First or Second Division. Mohawks emerged as First Division Champions, with Kelvingrove top of the Second.

There was a problem, however, in that with only one rink available ice time per team was severely curtailed. Doonside therefore agreed to disband and their players were absorbed into other teams. This process gradually continued, until by 1935–36 there were only five clubs in the League: Kelvingrove, Glasgow Lions, Glasgow Mustangs, Glasgow University and Glasgow Mohawks. Since 1930 there had been only one Division and the Championship had been shared equally between Kelvingrove, Mohawks and Bridge of Weir, each with two wins apiece.

From early on a policy of encouraging young home-grown talent had been followed and a Canadian coach employed for this purpose. That Scots had a natural bent for the game was well illustrated by Billy Fullerton. He was fast (as was only to be expected from a British speed-skating champion) but he was also a good backchecker, 'as good as any Canadian,' said his admirers. Other good Scottish players included Billy's brothers, John, who played centre for Mohawks and was also captain, and Alec, a defenceman with Kelvingrove. Glasgow policeman Dave Cross, Kelvingrove's goalie, was considered to be one of the safest in the business and had more than fifty representative games to his credit; and Joe Collins, later to play on defence for Great Britain, MacDonald, Montford and Glen Braid were other bright lights.

Most of these players of the 1930s, Scots and Canadians, were to be in the game for a long time. Sid Montford, a Glasgow newspaperman, was also 'Scotia' of *Ice Hockey World*, and Johnnie Kelly also contributed to the sport's own newspaper. Later Kelly became a radio and TV reporter and eventually returned to Canada in that capacity. Don Cumming was another who did well in the media, becoming a top TV producer. Rather appropriately for a policeman dour Dave Cross became a referee, whilst R.O. MacDonald became Secretary of the Scottish Ice Hockey Association.

The Scots picked up quite a few tips from the Canadians who played alongside them. Johnny Kelly (Mustangs) was a good stick-handler and an artiste with the poke-check, rarely seen these days; 18-year-old Wally Welch (Mohawks) packed a terrific shot and was an enterprising and forceful attacker; and there was a wily old veteran from Port Arthur, Ontario, in Jim Kenny, who both played and coached.

The season of 1935–36 saw many matches played against English teams, in addition to Scotland v. England. The Manchester squad were old opponents and there were some thrilling matches with them. The Mancunians beat a Glasgow Select, 2–1, 7–4, and 8–4, drew 5–5 with Scots Canadians (who, despite the name, included some of the Fullerton clan) and beat them 8–2. Birmingham Maple Leafs defeated Mohawks 13–2.

These might sound depressing results for Scottish hockey, but, in fact, Manchester had some very good players in high-scoring Les Tapp, who later played in Scotland; goalminder Scotty Palfrey, also Scotland-bound; and English international Johnson. Tapp, with Johnson and Stevenson, formed a smooth line which was quite accustomed to playing 60 minutes of a game. Moreover, in some of these matches they were reinforced by the Wembley player Sammy Gigliotti and another who was to be a hit north of the Border, George McWilliams. As for Birmingham Maple Leafs, they were the strongest combination in England outside the National League, with a nearly all-Canadian line-up. A number of their players eventually joined Scottish clubs.

The drawn game with Manchester was a thriller. Icing only seven men – Palfrey, Kochman, Gattiker, Edwards, Tapp, Johnson and Stevenson – Manchester trailed 5–4 until the final minute when Stevenson equalised. Billy Fullerton (3), W. Mac-Donald, a medical student at Edinburgh University who hailed from Canada, and Johnnie Kelly scored for the Scots. It was a pretty rough game, and the fact that Manchester's 'Magnificent Seven' came back to draw illustrates what 'iron men' there were in the game.

All in all, it was the best season yet in Scotland and it ended with Johnnie Kelly scoring a goal in eight seconds, Mohawks winning the Championship, and Kelvingrove taking the Boys' League. A satisfied SIHA asked official coach Graham Fraser, of Halifax, to return in 1936–37. He had replaced Pat Aitken, of Calgary, who had been coach the previous season.

Glasgow Mohawks were Champions again the next season, but with the construction of the Central Scotland Ice Rink at Perth and the entry of Perth Panthers into the League the wind of change was blowing through Scottish hockey. The new rink was purpose-built with seats for 2,500 plus standing accommodation, and at the head of operations was a very shrewd man, Adam Alexander.

The Perth project was a success from the start, not least because the shining new Panthers had their own version of 'The Two Leslies' – Les Tapp and Les Lovell. Tapp took his scoring habits from Manchester to Perth, and Lovell became an immortal, founding a Scottish hockey dynasty with sons and grandsons playing the game. Fifty years on there would be Lovells in British international teams and in the line-up of a famous club yet to come in 1936–37, Murrayfield Racers.

Tapp's story was not to have such a happy ending. Born in

Ottawa around 1913, he played in the Ottawa Industrial League before coming to England to join Birmingham Maple Leafs. He moved on to Manchester where he continued as a prolific scorer, not least against Scottish sides, and was snapped up by Perth. As with so many, the Second World War came along and interrupted his career at its peak. Afterwards, he and his wife Pat, whom he married while playing with Perth, opened a very successful flower shop at Walton-on-Thames, south of London. A quiet and unassuming man, he retained his interest in ice hockey and always kept in touch. One morning he was out in his car making some business calls when he felt ill. He pulled into the side of the road and died, a relatively young man.

That, thank Heaven, was a long way off as Les and Les paraded their not inconsiderable talent in the Perth cause. Public reaction to the new rink accelerated plans for other arenas, and with Perth determined to get good players the Glasgow teams also had to put on their thinking caps. There was a disagreement at the Cup Final between Mustangs and Lions. After a dispute over unregistered players, Mustangs refused to take the ice and Lions were awarded the Cup by default.

As a direct result of this, the SIHA insisted that for 1937–38 all players on every team must be properly registered with the Association and that players moving from the control of another Association should be legally transferred. The Glasgow directors were also forced to realise that they were not an island and with other rinks and other clubs coming on the scene they would no longer be able to lay down the law. One consequence was that, for the first time, they allowed twenty-minute periods at Crossmyloof, something they had hitherto refused to do.

Meanwhile, fired by Panthers' first season, Perth decided to ice a second team, Black Hawks. Les Tapp stayed with Panthers who recruited Len M'Cartney, star player of Glasgow Lions, and Bert Forsyth and 'Red' Thomson, who had been playing in England. Lovell moved across to lead the Black Hawks, where the line-up included the colourful Art Schumann, from Birmingham Maple Leafs, and Bob Purdie, from Brighton.

Against these useful Canucks, most of the Glasgow clubs remained unchanged. The champions, Mohawks, had signed a Scots-born Canadian, George Baillie, to replace Gordon Galloway who had moved on. Baillie would be around in British hockey for a long time. Otherwise, they relied on Palfrey in goal, defenceman Archie Bogie, forward Glen Braid and the Fullerton trio, John, Alec and Billy.

Kelvingrove, winners of the 1936–37 Coronation Cup, had

no Canadians at all although Cross (goal), Dick, Maxwell and Cuthill had all played in Canada as youngsters. They also had Johnston and Montford and welcomed back Ken Hurll who had been playing in Germany after a stint at Oxford University.

Johnny Kelly was the one bright star in the Mustangs line-up since Braid had gone to Mohawks and they had lost Russell to Lions. Lions had one effective line in Wally Welch, Stevenson and Kenny, but were pinning hopes on Archie Purdie, brother of Perth's Bob, and Jimmy Muir, a youngster with Canadian experience. But when Perth teams scored 23 goals in two games, the writing was on the wall. Panthers beat Lions 15−3, at that time a record in Scotland, and the Crossmyloof directors decided that the Glasgow clubs must be given help to strengthen their teams.

There were quite a few nomadic Canadians available to help, and express trains between London and Glasgow frequently carried hockey players. Lions signed Frank Chase and Bunt Roberts; Kelvingrove came up with 'Scotty' Cameron; Ney and Morrison signed with Mustangs. Others followed. Marchant came on spec and was signed by Mustangs. Mohawks signed McCaffrey, but then the player said he wanted to go back to London. Kelvingrove lost Dean Steadman to Switzerland, but replaced him with 20-year-old Don McLeod who made a sensational debut – he registered a goal and an assist and ended up in hospital where a mouth wound was stitched. Perhaps the most significant signing of all was goaltender 'Buster' Amantea, formerly with Wembley Canadians, who lined-up with Lions and proceeded to guard his net brilliantly. Perth were not idle meanwhile and Black Hawks were strengthened on defence by the acquisition of ex-Leaf 'Bill' Smith.

The standard of hockey was improving, but Sid Montford commented sadly that of about 100 Scots who had been playing with Glasgow teams in 1930, only three were still active – Johnny Fullerton, Andy Dick and himself. There were some good local youngsters coming along, however, especially at Perth where Alexander was encouraging youth and giving ice time to two Perth Academy teams. Tommy McInroy, Freddie Hill, Dougie Mitchell and 'Mac' Ross were amongst the newcomers who would make their mark.

The headlines, though, went mostly to Perth senior players. Milne, not content with playing well in goal for Panthers, also turned out as goalkeeper for the reserves of Perth's Scottish Football League club St Johnstone, and became the idol of two sets of fans. Les Tapp was the top goal-scorer on the circuit, and Panthers and Black Hawks remained almost unbeatable. The

Hawks finally succumbed to Glasgow Lions 4–3, largely due to a hat trick from Frank Chase. Chase had been with Wembley Canadians in 1935–36 and it is interesting to see that of that squad Amantea, Milne, Morrison, Shannon, Forsythe and McWilliams, as well as Chase, all eventually played in the Scottish League.

Milne was one of hockey's characters. Ronald, as he was christened, was born in Scotland and for eleven years lived next door to Crossmyloof before the family went to Canada. He came back to play soccer and was on Glasgow Rangers' books when he heard that ice hockey was being played in London. He went south and was signed by Wembley then loaned to Richmond Hawks when Clem 'Turkey' Harnedy went home in mid-season. During the 1935–36 season he was back at Wembley where chances were limited, Art Child being the regular netman for Lions and Amantea for Canadians. In the 1936–37 season Milne moved to Harringay but found himself in a worse position with Jimmy Foster minding the nets for Greyhounds and equally sound Andy Goldie for Racers. Milne, the best back-up goalie in the business, welcomed the opportunity to be his own man in Perth. He also married, the bride being Betty Deans, a high-scoring centre with one of the Perth womens' ice hockey teams.

'Scotty' Milne played in goal for Perth's ice hockey Panthers and football team St Johnstone.

A great season for 'Scottie' ended with Panthers just beating Black Hawks for the championship and ending Glasgow Mohawks' two year run. It didn't all go Perth's way, however. In a two-game series Glasgow beat Perth for the Simpson Trophy, and early in the season there was a surprise result when Glasgow defeated Birmingham Maple Leafs 2–0 and the next night the Leafs beat Perth 3–2. The Glasgow line-up on 12 November 1937, when the match was broadcast by the BBC was: Palfrey (goal); Bunt Roberts and Sid Forsythe (defence); Welch, Morrison and Kenny, first line; Chase, Baillie and Stevenson, second line. The goals were scored by Roberts and Chase.

Scottish hockey was broadening its outlook and an All Star team toured Germany later that season. It comprised Amantea (goal); Horne, Roberts and Bogie (defence); Billy Fullerton, Baillie, Marchant, Kelly, Chase, Purdie and Kenny (forwards). An invitation from the BIHA to send five Scottish players to try out for the British World Championship team was, however, understandably declined. The BIHA specified the positions required which meant that players like Billy Fullerton were automatically excluded.

A psychological blow was delivered when Brighton Tigers

crushed Perth All Stars 10–2 before 3,200 spectators, but was countered on 11 March 1938 when the Scottish League drew 1–1 with the World Champions, Sudbury Wolves, representing Canada. Again, the BBC covered the match, but despite this there was a capacity crowd. The game was scoreless through two periods, but in the third big Arnie Pratt (Panthers and formerly with Philco Radio alias Perivale Rovers) gave the Scots the lead with eight minutes remaining. Allan, a veteran who had previously toured Europe with Toronto Dukes, equalised three minutes from time. The Scottish League team on this occasion was: Amantea (goal), Roberts, Horne, Lovell and 'Biff' Smith (defence), Purdie, Stevenson and Baillie (first line), Pratt, Marchant and M'Cartney (second line). Tapp would undoubtedly have played had he not been injured.

The scene was now set for the biggest season yet in Scottish ice hockey. 1938–39 would see a truly national Scottish League with the two most famous Glasgow clubs, Mohawks and Kelvingrove, pitted against Perth Panthers (the management had decided against running two teams) and three newcomers, Dundee Tigers, Fife Flyers (based at Kirkcaldy) and Falkirk Lions.

The SIHA, whilst naturally not adverse to expansion, was anxious to see that Scots born-and-bred players were not crowded out. Accordingly, a limit of six Canadians was applied, the three new clubs who had not had the opportunity to develop home-grown talent being allowed seven. Thus, on paper at any rate, the six League outfits represented the strongest line-up of puck-chasers ever seen in Scotland.

Panthers, the defending champions, had Milne, Roberts, Schumann, Tapp, Bob Purdie, Pratt, Scott, Jimmy Allan and Norrie Andrew.

Mohawks, twice previously champions, had Palfrey, Horne, Bogie, McPherson, Cumming, Baillie, Shires, Dawson and Morrison.

Kelvingrove relied on Cross, Bert Forsythe, Joe Collins (a talented young Scottish defenceman), Nevatt, Cameron, Cadieux, Eaton, McLeod, Stacey and Marchant.

Fife Flyers had Kerr, Stover, Lovell, Alec Fullerton, Durling, McQuade, Billy Fullerton, M'Cartney and Olympic star Jimmy Chappell.

Falkirk Lions had another Olympic star, Gerry Davey, 'Chuck' Stapleford, McWilliams, Amantea, Gordie Pantalone (a defence recruit from Streatham), 'Red' Thomson, Russell and McMillan.

Dundee Tigers had Bruce Thompson (Bristol Bombers) in

goal, George McNeil (ex-Richmond and Earls Court), Merrick Cranstoun (ex-Earls Court) and 'Biff' Smith on defence, and Al Rogers (ex-Brighton), Jimmy Shannon, Lightfoot, Bryce and Cummings up-front. Thompson didn't settle and went back to Bristol, but Dundee secured in his place Bill Lane, from Birmingham Maple Leafs, a goalie who the experts had been saying for years was worth his place in a top League team. He had even been considered for the international squad.

Kelvingrove and Falkirk were further reinforced with Art Seafred and Nelson M'Cuaig respectively, but at the end of the season it would be the powerful newcomers, Dundee Tigers, who would come out on top.

The Falkirk rink officially opened in November 1938, the Lions set off on a winning streak and little Gerry Davey was the idol of the crowds. Perth's Tapp, however, remained the most popular player in Scotland, leading a poll throughout most of the season.

A new rink opened at Ayr in March 1939, and the Canadian World Champions, Trail Smoke Eaters, gave Scottish fans a hockey treat during a short, undefeated tour. Not that there was any disgrace in losing to Trail, who were probably the best Canadian 'amateur' team ever to visit Britain. They rampaged through Europe undefeated and untied for more than fifty games and it was not until the end of their tour when they came up against the star-stacked Harringay All Stars (with whom they drew 2–2) and Wembley All Stars (the only team to beat them: score 4–1) that they lost their proud record.

The SIHA and the BIHA finally sank some of their differences, and Billy Fullerton (Fife), Tommy McInroy (Fife) and Joe Collins (Kelvingrove) were amongst those chosen for the Great Britain team to take part in the World and European Championships. It was a long-deserved honour for Fullerton who, incidentally, disdained modern hockey tubes and preferred the old-fashioned 'automobile skate.'

All in all, the 1938–39 season seemed to be heralding a great future for the game. It is true that there were one or two small clouds on the horizon, like the fact that the English National League was still of a higher standard, but with giant stadiums like Wembley, Harringay and Earls Court, that was to be expected. Just the same, there was great disappointment in November 1938 when a Scottish All Star team comprising Amantea (goal), Pantalone, Roberts and McNeil (defence), Davey, Rogers, Cadieux, 'Breezy' Thompson, Schumann and M'Cartney (forwards) crashed 9–1 to London All Stars, who, despite the billing, included three Brighton men. The English

Two smart centremen who powered London All Stars to a 9–1 win over Scottish League All Stars: veteran Wally Monson (top) and the young Steve Latoski (bottom).

team was: Goldie (goal), Gillies, Shewan and Keane (defence), 'Red' Stapleford, Archer, Poirier, Aubuchon, Latoski and Monson (forwards). Stapleford (3), Latoski, Aubuchon, Monson, Keane, Archer and Shewan were the scorers, with 'Breezy' Thompson making a lone reply.

Another small cloud came when the SIHA fined Glenn Morrison and Len M'Cartney £2 each for fighting. 'How can you impose cash penalties on amateurs?' asked the Press. A good question; but the SIHA, undeterred, fined other 'amateurs' in their bid to keep the game clean.

The biggest cloud of all was a cloud over the world. As Scotland prepared for an even better season in 1939–40, a mad Austrian house-painter was about to plunge the whole world into chaos.

Don Cumming, who became a top producer with Scottish Television, has vivid memories of the game's growth in Scotland. Taken to Canada at two years of age he returned from Montreal at 15 and was astonished to find that Glasgow Mohawks were prepared to pay him to play ice hockey. Apart from appearing in the Montreal Forum as a 12-year-old in the Quebec schools play-offs, he had never seen artificial ice before. From Mohawks he went to Ayr and its magnificent new stadium and then to Falkirk, which had a strong team including Gerry Davey, Tommy Forgie and two of the three Beaton brothers, Bobby and Clem.

During the early war years many exhibition games were played, and Don, awaiting call-up to the Air Force, was appointed coach at Paisley where he had players like Tommy Lauder, Billy Bodnar and Ken Nicholson. Some of the matches were against Canadian Service teams with NHL players in their ranks.

Don lost two teeth and broke a collar-bone in a match at Dundee and went off to war suitably prepared. Demobbed in 1945 he was astounded to learn that the SIHA, under their new recruiting system, were barring all their pre-war players (a policy sensibly changed later). He took up refereeing and eventually was contracted to run the refereeing set-up, personally handling four to six games per week. Journalism and broadcasting eventually led him into television, where he has, like Alan Weeks in England, always done his best for ice hockey.

Don's favourite hockey story is of a tragedy that had a happy ending. Let him tell it his way:

'About 1956, a young hockey player, Gus Galbraith, newly married, came over with his wife, Lorraine. He played only a couple of games and one night at Paisley had a bad fall – so bad that a leg had to be amputated. He came from Timmins, Ontario, where Roy Thomson (later Lord Thomson) set up his first radio station. I made an approach to Thomson to help launch a radio appeal over his entire Canadian network and his Press empire on both sides of the Atlantic. The response was tremendous and Gus Galbraith, instead of returning home, stayed in Britain to take a BSc degree at Strathclyde University.

'Gus is now retired and he and Lorrie live on Vancouver Island in a clearing surrounded by pines and Douglas firs, with a salmon stream flowing past the back door. A near-neighbour is the Mayor of Nanaimo, Frank Ney, who played in Glasgow before the war and is a reputed millionaire from real estate.'

Forty-five years on and England score nine to Scotland's three in an international at Durham.

6 THEY SHOOT – THEY SCORE

The days of youth tend to take on a rosy glow in later years, and to me the 1930s were golden years in ice hockey. To my brother and I, the players of Richmond Hawks and Earls Court Rangers were heroes, and when Harringay Arena opened and a sport-mad father came home with tickets for all the family, ice hockey had two more very ardent supporters (Mother refused to become a convert). To a parent who was a good all-round sportsman himself, watching was not enough and soon skates were added to the mass of sports equipment which was poor Mother's despair. Mine were double runners, goalie's skates – which as I couldn't skate very well but never wanted to play anywhere save in goal, was just as well. There was no containing the enthusiasm of Dad and when the professionals – Detroit Red Wings and Montreal Canadiens – came to England, the Drackett family were there again.

Memories of those schoolboy days are crystal-clear today. The hockey in the English National League was probably the best in the world outside the professional National Hockey League which, at that time, had only seven teams: Montreal Canadiens, Toronto Maple Leafs, Detroit Red Wings, Boston Bruins, Chicago Black Hawks, New York Rangers and Brooklyn Americans, the latter soon to follow Montreal Maroons into oblivion. That this was so was demonstrated by the number of English players who subsequently played professionally in the NHL, AHL and USHL, or senior 'amateur' in the Quebec Hockey League, then rated the best league in Canada.

Then there was Britain's triumph in the Olympics; the World Championships in London; the foundation of the world's first ice hockey publication, *Ice Hockey World*; and so much more besides. I remember queues at Harringay for the World Championships winding twice around the giant building, and an enterprising salesman chanting, 'Telfer's hot pies' as people shivered and stamped their feet in the cold night air. It is not just a case of memory holding the door, they truly were golden years.

The catalyst was the opening in 1934 of the Empire Pool & Sports arena at Wembley, which would be followed by Empress Hall, Earls Court, and then Harringay – three great arenas of which, alas, only Wembley survives. The man behind the Empire Pool was Norwich-born Arthur Elvin (later Sir Arthur), who from humble beginnings in a tobacco kiosk at the Empire Exhibition, Wembley, became one of the biggest sports promoters in the world and head man of Wembley Stadium as well as the Pool. The Pool, which as the name implies, was also intended for major swimming events, was the first rink to be built in the United Kingdom with a full-size ice pad and seating accommodation – around 10,000 – suitable for international events. Nothing but the best was good enough for Elvin and he expected the highest standards from his players, both on and off the ice.

The new Lions and Canadians reflected that attitude. Gerry Cosby was in goal for Lions, 'Buster' Amantea for Canadians. Cosby later returned to Europe as goalminder of the US national team, and the Gerry Cosby sports store still advertises in the NHL programme of New York Rangers. 'Buster' was later to be rated Scotland's top goalie. Lions also recruited Gordon Dailley from Grosvenor House and two top forwards in Bobby Walton and Edgar Murphy. The long and lanky Murphy, affectionately known as 'Spud', suffered one of the worst accidents in a British rink when one skate lodged in the boards at Harringay and the other sliced through a tendon. There was blood on the ice and 'Spud' was out for a long time.

Canadians had British speed-skater Bob Wyman, Glenn Morrison (who, like several others, originally worked his way over on a cattle-boat and later starred in Scottish hockey), another who did well in Scotland in due course, George McWilliams, and a fellow who was to end up in Canada's Hall of Fame, Jake Milford. On defence was a young man named Clarence 'Sonny' Rost who, like Les Lovell in Scotland, was to found a hockey dynasty with son and grandson to follow in his footsteps.

Of all the colourful players Wembley signed, however, none could match the charisma of the Lions' captain, 'Lou' Bates, voted most popular athlete in Ottawa Valley. He had toured Europe with Ottawa Shamrocks in 1933–34 and finished out the season in Paris with Français Volants. In 1934 he came to Wembley and a new star was born. Tall, dark and good-looking, 'Lou' brought the crowds – men and women – to their feet with his spectacular rushes down the ice. The cry of 'Lou-oo-oo-oo' echoed through the stadiums, and newcomers would ask why the big Wembley defenceman was being booed. Advertising agents booked his services, he appeared in films, and he brought a powerful image to a sport which badly needed personalities to sell itself to a new public. Bates was one of the

'Mr Ice Hockey' of the 1930s 'Lou' Bates, captain of Wembley Lions, a photo taken from a cigarette card which indicates his popularity.

'Lou' as he is today, with a star of post-war hockey, George Beach.

best ever to play in Britain. He was a good player with that extra something, the something which makes the crowds flock to see a Georgie Best, an Ian Botham or a Muhammad Ali. He was to play in Britain for many years and became a coach when his playing days were done. As this book is written, he is still alive and well and living in Wembley. The black hair and the moustache are silver now, but the charisma remains.

'Lou' was not the only player the fans had to shout about. The two Paris clubs, largely staffed by flamboyant French-Canadians, played against the English teams in an International Club Tournament, and Munich, Prague and Davos also visited Britain. The favourite visitors were World Champions Canada, represented by a great bunch of puck-chasers, Winnipeg Monarchs, some of whom would return to play here. It was an indication of the strength of English squads that Monarchs, although winning one match against England and beating

Streatham 1–0, lost another to England and were beaten twice by Wembley.

The League was no push-over for one of the Wembley teams. Richmond Hawks had a good, Canadian-dominated line-up, and Streatham had quietly recruited some outstanding Canucks to weld with their experienced British players. The South London rink signed 'Bobby' Giddens from Paris as player-coach, Maurice Gerth, a big goalie whose baseball slides were to the despair of many an opposing forward, and George Shaw and Harvey 'Red' Stapleford, two rugged high-scoring forwards. Added to home-based Carl Erhardt, Ernie Ramus, Pete Halford, Ralph Couldrey and Gerry Davey, this gave Streatham the best-balanced team in the circuit, and in due course they took the Championship and the International Club Tournament for good measure, Canadians having the consolation of winning both the London and Channel Cups.

A remarkable feature of the championship team was that every one of them made their mark on British hockey as players, coaches, administrators, journalists or combinations thereof.

Wembley Canadians owed much of their more limited success to the 'Three M' line of Glenn Morrison, Jake Milford and George McWilliams. They too had important roles to play.

Another who played in the first match at Wembley in 1934 and went on playing until he was 51, Clarence 'Sonny' Rost, who was presented with a silver salver after his thousandth game in Wembley colours.

The following season, 1935–36, was to be bigger and better. Freddie Summerhayes, the man who introduced Grosvenor

Bob Giddens, who launched the world's first ice hockey newspaper, *Ice Hockey World*, in 1935, seen with another Hall of Fame member, centre Joe Beaton, of Richmond, Harringay and Wembley.

House Canadians, had constructed an ice rink in the Earls Court Exhibition grounds, taking a leaf out of Elvin's book. Empress Hall had a very large ice surface and seating accommodation for more than 7,000 spectators. A comfortable stadium, some of the red plush and atmosphere of theatre lingered on. It brought two new teams into the League, Earls Court Rangers and the exotically named Kensington Corinthians.

Brighton, too, had a new rink, the Sports Stadium, with Hammersmith and Richmond impresario, Claude Langdon, on the board. Although the ice surface was not as big as Empress Hall, it was the recommended size for ice hockey, 185 feet by 85 feet. Spectator capacity was 3,000. The Sports Stadium opened on 26 October 1935 and introduced the Tigers, a team which was to have a long and illustrious history.

Lord Decies officially opened Empress Hall a month later. Summerhayes pulled out all the publicity stops and put up the Empress Cup, for which Corinthians defeated Rangers 2–1. Corinthians flattered to deceive, although most of their troubles were not of their own making. Giddens had been lured from Streatham as player-coach and the Cup-winning line-up looked more than promising. 'Jock' Riddell, born in Mearns, Scotland, a wanderer in the Depression whose motto was 'Have skates, will travel', was a revelation in goal, and Giddens always thought he got a raw deal by not being selected for the British Olympic team that season. Other Corinthians included Alec Higginson, 'Scotty' Cameron, a very highly-rated Gar Preston and Ernie Gathercole.

The first big blow for the new team came when Splaine, Harris and Gallagher, all American citizens, were refused work permits by the Home Office. In vain did Earls Court argue that they were playing as amateurs; the Home Office would not be moved. Some of the other players were injured, and there was dissension between Giddens and the management. The coach had launched *Ice Hockey World* during the season and with hindsight it seems reasonable to assume that it took up time which the Corinthians could have utilised. Troubles proliferated, and one night a senior Earls Court official approached Giddens with words of criticism just as the player-coach was leaving the ice. Anyone with any sense would know better than to raise such matters with a hockey player, hot, tired and disappointed at the end of a losing game. Words led to blows, and Giddens resigned as coach.

The management were reluctant to lose him as a player – he was a good centreman or winger with a wristy and powerful shot – and he was transferred to the Rangers. It was an unsatisfactory situation, and after a while he quit to devote all his energies to his newspaper. It was the sport's gain, because *Ice Hockey World* played a major role in promoting ice hockey in Great Britain.

The other new club at Empress Hall had better luck and, it could be argued, better players. Ran 'Ace' Forder was a very sound goalie and he had in front of him (at least, when they were not occupying the penalty-box) two big bustling defence-men of whom we have already heard, McAlpine and MacPhail. Amongst the forwards there was real genius in that 'dapper Dan' of centres, Don Willson, and a winger rated in Canada as the world's outstanding amateur, Johnny Acheson. With Gates, Hodges and those two hustling business men, together in work and play, Jimmy Chappell and Howie Peterson, Rangers not surprisingly had the highest-scoring attack in the League. Alas, not all the forwards skated both ways and, as referees got arm-ache jerking their thumbs at the two 'Scotties', Forder sometimes lacked protection.

Brighton's great days were also to come. The original squad turned out not much better than the Corinthians. A lack of experience of English conditions probably hampered what seemed a reasonable line-up. Captained by Bobby Beaton, brother of the more famous Joe, and who afterwards went to Scotland, Tigers had a good goalie in Leo Sargent, who later went to Richmond, a clever centre in 'Toad' Klein, who would continue in the League with Harringay and Wembley, bustling little Hymie McArthur, another wanderer of the Great Ice Way, and some big, bouncing gentlemen like defenders Harry Pyefinch and Clyde Nears, forwards Bill and George Parsons and the versatile Jimmy Borland. Only the Corinthians conceded more goals than Tigers, and the latter's goal tally of 49 was the lowest in the land. Despite this the 'House Full' signs were often up at the Sports Stadium.

The star players were mostly with the two Wembley teams, Richmond Hawks and the reigning champions, Streatham. The latter were built around Gerth, Stapleford, Shaw, Davey and Erhardt again. Runners-up the previous season, Canadians had a pretty experienced bunch in Amantea, Morrison, Milford, McWilliams, Sid Forsythe, Frank Chase, Jim Templeton, and a giant and effective blocker, Jack Wilkinson, a pal of 'Lou' Bates from Ottawa.

Lions hardly had a weakness, although Art Child in the nets was a long way from the best in the League, but Lions had 'Scottie' Milne as insurance in that department, and from goal out it was one of the most powerful combinations ever iced. 'Lou' Bates and Des Smith (who later played in the NHL) were astride the blue-line, and the first line of attack had Tony Lemay centring his brother Albert and Bobby Walton, two of the best wingers in the British game's history. The second line had Alec Archer, Jack Kilpatrick and Gordon Dailley or, if the versatile Dailley was needed on defence, Sammy Gigliotti.

Hawks, guided by Percy Nicklin, were hardly less powerful. Foster in the nets had in front of him two of the toughest defencemen in the League: Frank Currie, who later played with Harringay Greyhounds and Earls Court Rangers, and Len Godin, later with Paris, Manchester Rapids and Wembley Monarchs. Godin, from the mining town of Timmins, Ontario, was good enough to have been offered a try-out with Montreal. Currie is still active in hockey today as a scout for the Toronto Maple Leafs. Hawks' redoubtable forwards included Joe Beaton, the brothers Earl and Ivor Nicholson, 'Duke' Campbell,

Streatham 1935–36. League Champions the previous season, this powerful combination failed to keep the title by one point. Left to right: Dunbar Poole (manager), Gerry Davey, Archie Stinchcombe, Frank Trottier, 'Dickie' von Trauttenberg, George Shaw, Carl Erhardt (captain), 'Babe' Donnelly (player-coach), Ernie 'Al' Batson, Bobby Hales, Tommy Durling, 'Red' Stapleford, George Bourner (trainer) R.J. Buck (assistant manager). In front: Maurice Gerth.

'Chirp' Brenchley and Johnny Coward. They also had English internationals, Neville Melland and Major W.H. Mackenzie. Canadian-born Mackenzie, who had played for London Lions for a long time, was Hawks' manager and the oldest player in the League at 42.

Rarely has there been a closer struggle for the Championship. Lions edged out Hawks on goal average – 96 to 54 against 83 to 52 – and Streatham were only one point behind. Canadians were fourth, two points behind the South Londoners. It was a grand season and Britain's Olympic triumph was something more than icing on the cake.

The advent of Harringay Arena provided yet another boost for the 1936–37 campaign. Suddenly the League found itself with eleven clubs instead of seven. The inclusion of Harringay Racers and Greyhounds had been planned, but Southampton Vikings and Manchester Rapids came into being by accident. The two teams had started the season as Français Volants and Sports Club Rapide de Paris, but the Paris management ran into financial difficulties and decided to close down their hockey activities. A combined operation involving the BIHA, Southampton and Manchester rinks and the managements of Wembley and Harringay led to both clubs crossing the Channel and joining the English National League. They brought variety, colour and speed to the circuit but their performances were very erratic. Most of them were French-Canadians who found Southampton and Manchester a poor substitute for 'Gay Paree', and their play suffered accordingly.

Rapids had a spectacular netman in Johnny Lacelle, afterwards with Valleyfield Braves; two beautiful play-making centres in Larry Laframboise and Dick Proulx and winger Frankie Cadorette, later snapped up by Wembley. The rugged Mr Godin was on defence, with veteran 'Dollar' Belhumeur and Harringay-loaned George Pearson to complete the blue-line trio.

Vikings lost a player or two in the transition from Paris but they had men of the calibre of Tony Demers, whose wicked shot from the wing was to earn him an NHL slot (at one time he was said to have the most powerful shot in hockey anywhere); a centre with a fine Canadian reputation, who was a very prolific scorer, Hugh Farquharson; and another good winger, Theo Hamel.

The defence was an odd sight to British fans. Philbin and Landymore had the build of all-in wrestlers and, wearing helmets of the type popular with racing cyclists, they looked like two terrifying giant crabs. Behind them 'Kick' McCann was an elongated question mark in a baseball cap. Reinforcements were needed and Wembley provided Amantea (goal), Horne (defence) and Wally Rost, brother of Sonny (forward).

The two Harringay clubs proved power-houses from the start, and intense rivalry grew up between them and their North London rivals at Wembley. Nicklin had picked well. Foster, Brenchley, Currie, Campbell and the Nicholson brothers had moved with him from Richmond. To them he added hockey luminaries such as Winnipeg's Walter 'Pop' or 'Fox' Monson, a great centre who had been on the 1932 Canadian Olympic Championship team and winger Archie Creighton. Several of his choices would in due course play professional hockey – Wib 'Dutch' Hiller and Joe Shack (New York Rangers), Dick Adolph (Cleveland Barons) and Bob Whitelaw (Detroit Red Wings) among them. Len Burrage, a cagey stick-handling rearguard (who 'Bob' Giddens thought the best defenceman ever to play in Britain) would, in his veteran years, break all scoring records for defencemen in the US Eastern Amateur League. His 61 points and 48 assists in 1940–41 were not surpassed until the 1955–56 season. Then there was Dunc Cheyne, 'Curly' Kerr, 'Toad' Klein (from Brighton), Jake Brunning, 'Fan' Heximer and Bob McCranor, many of whom would play major roles in British hockey.

There was also Bert Peer, a man once described as his own worst enemy. There have been few better right-wingers. A big bull-necked man with a long easy stride, he was deceptively fast. At one time they used to have puck-chasing contests at Harringay, one circuit of the ice pad passing behind both goals and keeping the puck under control. Peer looked so slow that the crowd was urging him to 'get a move on', but in fact he equalled the fastest time, around fourteen seconds as I recall. His strength enabled him to shake off the huskiest defender and let loose a vicious shot. He later played minor pro with Omaha, Fort Worth and Tulsa but never made the NHL grade, perhaps because of his temperament.

There was only one team good enough to put the newcomers in their place and that was the reigning champions, Wembley Lions. They had substantially their title-winning team back again but with one or two positions strengthened. Roy Musgrove had taken over in goal and he was a hard man to beat. One night his pads were measured and were found to be wider than the regulations allowed, but with narrower pads he still provided an iron curtain. He wore spectacles, protected by an eye mask, and an ordinary cap; goalies did not wear helmets or face-masks in those days.

Wembley Lions 1936–37, League Champions for the second year in succession. Left to right: Roy Musgrove, Albert Lemay, Tony Lemay, Jack Kilpatrick, Bobby Walton, Sammy Gigliotti, 'Jo-Jo' Grabowski, Alec Archer, 'Lou' Bates, Gordon Dailley, Cam Shewan, Edgar Murphy, A. Jackson (team manager).

Jacques Plante, of Montreal Canadiens, is generally considered to be the first netman to wear a mask and that was not until 1955 and then only in practice sessions. Four years later when he took the decision to wear a full face-mask in matches, Plante had already suffered 200 stitches, broken his nose four times, his cheekbones and jaw and had a hairline skull fracture. Even with the mask it was still dangerous. Plante suffered a loss of form and Coach 'Toe' Blake thought his vision was impaired by the mask. Plante shrugged his shoulders and said, 'I am too young to die.' Now 99 out of 100 goalies wear a mask.

The Lions' second line needed a little 'extra' (the Lemays and Walton were back on the first) and that was provided by a great character and fine hockey player in 'Jo-Jo' Grabowski. After the season started, defender Des Smith was switched to the other Wembley team, now rechristened Monarchs, but this scarcely weakened Lions as his replacement, Cam Shewan, was a sound blocker. Shewan, like the Lemay brothers and Harringay's Archie Creighton, had been a member of the great Winnipeg Monarchs' squad of 1934–35.

Monarchs were a useful team, but the main threat to Racers, Lions and Greyhounds came from Earls Court Rangers where hold-overs Forder, MacPhail, Willson, Acheson, Peterson and Preston had been joined by a dashing defenceman Harry Brown, another sound rearguard in Doug Maundrell and a very good winger, Jack Forsey. The League would end with Lions (62 points) champions again, Racers (59), Greyhounds (55) and Rangers (51).

Poor old Richmond, denuded of their stars by Harringay, had

Jack Keating, a lone Richmond star after most of the Hawks moved to Harringay. Eventually he would follow them before turning professional.

only Johnny Coward and Joe Beaton left of their squad, although they recruited a fine forward in Jack Keating and were joined later in the season by Tommy Forgie. Sargent, in goal, faced scores of pucks and had almost as many defencemen in front of him. Ham Riley, a fair good-looking giant, was more or less a regular fixture, but Hawks also used 'Biff' Smith, George McNeil, Jimmy Carr (back from Egypt), Bob Wyman and, eventually, Rudy Pilous, who was on the roster as a centre-ice. Rudy was a big man, though, and when Forgie, also a centre, was signed, Pilous moved back.

In September 1985 Pilous was inducted into the Canadian Hockey Hall of Fame. He coached Chicago Black Hawks to the Stanley Cup in 1961 and was General Manager of Winnipeg Jets when they won the World Hockey Association Avon Trophy in 1976 and 1978. Later he became Director of Operations, St Catherine's Saints, Toronto Maple Leafs' farm club – not bad for a fellow who never made pro himself!

The 197 goals which rattled into the Richmond nets during the League schedule were not to be compared with the 232 which Earls Court's other club conceded. The ill-fated Kensington Corinthians had been rechristened Earls Court Royals, but what's in a name?

Royals had a couple of bustling forwards, Bob Kirkpatrick, who later turned pro, and Ab Welsh, from Saskatoon Quakers, but Royals' main claim to fame was that they introduced two of the enduring names in British hockey, Gib Hutchinson and Henry Hayes.

After one season with the ill-starred Royals' 'Hutch' was working as a carpenter at the Earls Court Exhibition when he got the call to don a sweater for Rangers who needed strengthening in the nets. That call led to an illustrious career culminating in recognition as Britain's top goalie in the championship years of the post-war Brighton Tigers. He married a daughter of Bombardier Billy Wells, one-time British heavyweight champion, the man who used to hammer a gong on the credit titles of all Rank Organisation movies. Gib still lives in Sussex.

Henry Hayes, a hard worker in the cause of Earls Court and Streatham, later became coach of Fife Flyers when the original British League came into being. Henry was a very strict disciplinarian who expected, most of us would say quite rightly, one hundred per cent effort from his players. One night I was in Kirkcaldy with Harringay Racers and Flyers had not put up much resistance. In the visiting dressing-room after the match we heard the most tremendous noise from across the corridor.

Henry was laying down the law in no uncertain terms and in the voice of a regimental Sergeant-Major. We felt we were intruding on private grief.

After the Streatham debacle of 1939 which we will come to in due course, Henry played in Canada in the crack Quebec League with Sherbrooke Red Raiders and later coached Sydney Millionaires in the Cape Breton League, two circuits which featured many former English National League players.

When Earls Court Rangers returned to the ice in 1948, coach Kenny Campbell (not to be confused with 'Duke' Campbell who later coached Rangers) recruited Henry from Sydney, and Hayes brought with him a couple of other Millionaires, one of whom, Stan DeQuoy, was a big success in Britain, first with Rangers and then with Wembley Lions.

Coaching Rangers in those times was not a job for anyone looking for a long-service medal. I well remember Kenny Campbell, seated in the old Lyons Corner House just off Piccadilly Circus, pondering his future. In the event he left Earls Court after one season and joined his old pal, 'Red' Stapleford, at Streatham as a player. After retiring from hockey he died in tragic fashion. He was ploughing some land on his farm when the tractor overturned. Henry Hayes succeeded him as Rangers' coach but not for too long. Then he followed Kenny's path to Streatham before moving on to Scotland. In retirement he lives in Lachine, Province of Quebec.

1936–37 saw Streatham drop from their previous eminence to seventh place. The engine-room of the club – Stapleford, Davey, Shaw, Stinchcombe and Frank Trottier – was still powerful, but so many other clubs were stacked with stars. Whereas Streatham's new imports were never seen again, apart from Ches Dawson who moved north to the Scottish League. Erhardt and von Trauttenberg were still with the South London club they had served so well but they were nearing the end of their illustrious careers. Despite their troubles, Streatham did reach the final of the International Cup but lost in two straight games to Lions.

Interest in the World and European Championships played at Harringay and Wembley was at fever pitch, and the giant stadia were filled to capacity for all the important matches. Understandably, lesser lights such as Rumania played to three Embassy officials, two men and a dog in afternoon matches which were necessary to fit in a crowded schedule.

Great Britain had high hopes of retaining both World and European Championships. Nicklin was still coach and he had Foster, Erhardt, Dailley, Archer, Stinchcombe, Chappell,

Earls Court Royals' main claim to fame was that they introduced Henry Hayes (top) who was to play for Streatham, and be player-coach of EC Rangers and Fife Flyers (seen in Ranger uniform), and Gib Hutchinson (bottom), ace goalminder of Royals, Rangers, Wembley Lions and Brighton Tigers (in Brighton uniform).

Andy Goldie; in 1937 all three goalies chosen by Great Britain were playing for Harringay.

Davey, Brenchley and Coward remaining of the Olympic heroes. Rangers' Paul MacPhail had finally been forgiven and added vigour to the defence, and there was a welcome new centreman, diminutive jockey-capped Jimmy Kelly, from Brighton. The squad was rounded out by craggy winger Norm McQuade (Wembley Monarchs), a promising newcomer Jimmy Anderson (Earls Court Royals) and 'Scottie' Milne, now spare goalie to both Harringay teams, as stand-by backstop. On paper, at least, it looked a stronger team than the Olympic one.

Britain, in fact, picked three goalminders, all from the same rink. Foster, of Harringay Greyhounds, was automatically first choice and the original second selection was Andy Goldie, of Harringay Racers, a very good goalie indeed. There was little to choose between him and Foster, and it was British-born Andy's misfortune to be a contemporary with the great man. Racers were away on a tour whilst the Championships were on and Goldie, realistically assessing that his chances of playing in the Championships were nil unless Foster was hurt, asked to be allowed to go with his club. Milne was chosen in his place, thus making the Harringay goalies Britain's first, second and third choices.

Canada, thirsting for revenge, were represented by a tough bunch of puck-chasers from a tough mining town, Kimberley Dynamiters. They were taking no prisoners and no chances. Two of their top men from the previous season – Harry Brown and Jack Forsey – were now playing for Earls Court Rangers and the CAHA requested permission to use them. The BIHA gave permission for Forsey to play but revealed that Brown was under consideration for the British team – he was born in England. In the end, poor Brown did not play for either team: he was not allowed to play for Britain as he had been a member of the Canadian Championship team the year before, and he was not allowed to play for Canada because he was English. Britain could have done with him – he was a first-class defenceman and would have been a great help.

There were two key matches and both took place at Harringay. In the first, Great Britain played Canada, a meeting of the Titans. It was a stormy match, made worse by the incompetence of the Belgian referee, Popliment, a prominent hockey official for many years, whose decisions were incomprehensible to players and spectators alike. His worst efforts seemed to go against the home side and the crowd grew more and more ill-tempered until, after a particularly bad decision, they erupted, throwing programmes, newspapers, oranges and other missiles on the ice and bringing the game to a halt. An ugly situation was averted by quick thinking on the part of Charlie Tinn, leader of the Arena band. He struck up 'God Save The King', angry spectators duly stood to attention and the uproar died down. The game resumed with the Canadians winning 3–0, the only goals that Foster conceded throughout the tournament as he racked up eight shut-outs.

Switzerland were a power in hockey in those days, their lightly-built team playing a fast, skilful game, led by the famous 'Ni-sturm' line of the Cattini brothers and Torriani. When they skated out against Canada, both World and European titles were still in the balance. Great Britain had lost to Canada, Switzerland had lost to Great Britain. If the Swiss could now edge out Canada, all three teams would be tied. Hundreds of Swiss fans yelling 'Op Swees' found themselves supported by the locals, who not only had a vested interest in the outcome but also preferred the style of hockey played by Switzerland. It turned out to be the best match of the series, probably Switzerland's finest hour. They took the Dynamiters into overtime before losing 2–1. Thus Canada regained the World title and Great Britain had to be content with the European.

The season ended with a tournament created to attract extra interest in ice hockey, especially amongst the thousands of overseas visitors here for the Coronation of King George VI. It was named the Coronation Tournament.

The first round was contested between the two Harringay clubs, Monarchs, Streatham, Brighton and a combined Manchester–Southampton side under the title 'French–Canadian All Stars'. Wembley Lions, touring Canada, were given a bye into the second round where they were joined by Greyhounds, Streatham and Racers who had finished in that order in the first. Greyhounds, unbeaten with five wins in the first round, lost all three of their matches in the second and it was their co-tenants, Racers, who took the honours, with Lions second.

The flow of top players from Canada continued unabated in 1937–38 and there was no doubt that the English National League was the best in the world outside the professional ranks. What made them come here?

Gerry Heffernan, who came over that season to join Greyhounds, explains: 'Jobs were scarce then unless one had a trade, and money from hockey was just about enough to last for the five-month season. Most of us took whatever work was

Gerry Heffernan in his bench-warming days with Harringay Greyhounds (top) and his great years with the famous Montreal Canadiens (bottom).

available and lived carefully. Henry Hayes, after playing for Montreal Royals in the Junior League, went overseas and so did Johnny Taugher, Patsy Seguin, Frank Currie, Gordie Poirier, Jimmy Kelly, Frankie Leblanc and my very good and kind friend, Bobby Lee. But very few knew at that time what the English teams were paying for good Canadian players. We should have guessed when Jimmy Foster, goaltender for the Moncton Hawks, Allan Cup winners two years in succession, went over to England with Percy Nicklin. Most of his other team-mates turned professional (although mainly to the league one notch below the NHL). I can only recall Bill Miller going to the NHL Montreal Maroons and Montrealer Bert Connolley to New York Rangers. If I were a betting man I would wager that Jimmy Foster did better financially than the rest of his great team.

'When the word got around that the money was better in England there was no lack of players ready to make the trip, which somewhat annoyed the Canadian Amateur Hockey Association. English clubs were paying more than double that being paid in 'amateur' circles in Canada and the United States. A personal example: for my previous season with Montreal Royal Seniors (1936–37) I received $300 (£65). Harringay paid me £10 weekly, a total of about $1,100, for the season 1937–38. Many of the better and established players were on £12 weekly and higher. Johnny Acheson, from Toronto, played with Earls Court and I would guess that he was earning £20 weekly. Lester Patrick considered him to be the best player outside the NHL and Johnny never did turn pro. Coming back from England he joined the Royals and was on our team that lost to Port Arthur in 1938–39 in the Allan Cup Finals.

'Another attraction in addition to the money was to travel to England and France, get paid for a game we loved, visit the 'Old Country', meet new people and learn how others in far-off lands lived.

'My particular situation before accepting Nicklin's offer may or may not be typical. I was 20, my first year out of junior hockey, when I joined Montreal Royals in the fall of 1936. The League consisted of Quebec Aces, Ottawa Senators and four or five teams from in and around Montreal. Attendance at Sunday afternoon double-headers was on average 14,000. During the week, Wednesday night, it usually was about 8 to 10,000. Les Canadiens at the time were only drawing 3 to 5,000 on a Saturday night.

'Johnny Mahaffy (who later went to Streatham) centred Pete Morin and yours truly and we did fairly well. Buddy O'Connor had been playing a year ahead of us and was considered a professional prospect. The line which was to become famous as 'The Razzle Dazzle Line' only came into being when Mahaffy went overseas and O'Connor became our centre.

'In the spring of 1937 I worked as a clerk at $10 weekly in a stockbroker's office in Montreal. Word reached me that Lakeshore Goldminers in Kirkland Lake had jobs for hockey and baseball players, so I wrote to Bill Brydges, manager of the hockey team. Within ten days I was up in Northern Ontario earning $30 a week in the Assay Office. Having spent all my life in a big city like Montreal, Kirkland Lake was not my cup of tea – nor pot of gold. After three months, Buddy O'Connor sent me a letter he had received from Percy Nicklin offering him a contract to play over there.

'Buddy, being on the NHL list, was not allowed to go, and Pete Morin, having played a year in Chamonix in 1935–36, did not wish to leave Montreal again. I was third on the list, low man on the hockey stick, and that's how the invitation came my way. It offered £10 weekly and transportation. I wrote straight away to say I was interested and in September 1939 I sailed from Montreal with Bill Hogarth, from Fort William. Financially I was moving upwards, $10 weekly in the spring, $30 in the summer and $50 in the hockey season.

'The rest is history. As a bench-sitter at Harringay I deserved the Stanley/Allan cushion. The Greyhounds needed a centre-ice man, not Heffernan, the right-winger. Joe Beaton came in to fill the spot and he did a great job – married well too. (Joe married the daughter of tractor magnate Jack Olding; the family were regular spectators at Harringay.) The Harringay management with Major Mackenzie and Percy Nicklin were good to their hockey players and met all their obligations, even to someone like myself who played but a quarter of the schedule.

'On a beautiful autumn day, Hogarth and I were met at Euston Station by Nobby Clark, the trainer, and driven directly to the Arena. We were pleasantly surprised by what we saw – one of the best-planned sporting buildings I had ever seen. Montreal Forum, Quebec Colisée and Ottawa Auditorium were by comparison shabby and far behind Harringay.

'Good digs were easily found near the rink and at reasonable rates – 32s. per week for bed and board. Admittedly we missed central heating, but soon became used to the English climate. For a good woollen suit I paid 30s., the equivalent of $7.50. (In 1984 I paid £295 new money, 450 US dollars, for a hand-tailored sports jacket.) The Finsbury Park Empire, with top acts, was about 7s. 6d. Saveloys and ham rolls – and how tasty they

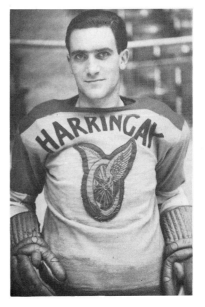

Billy Hogarth, who forgot he was not in Canada and stepped off a kerb looking the wrong way.

were – could be bought just outside the entrance to the rink, but I never did acquire the taste for jellied eels.

'Despite the little ice time I had, I never regretted going to England. On the contrary, it was the happiest time of my bachelor life and to top it all I met and married the most wonderful girl, London born-and-bred. I only wish that all Canadian hockey players were as fortunate as I have been in married life. In 1986 we made our thirtieth trip back to London, but it's always sad when I go by Harringay Stadium and see the old ice hockey arena occupied by a wholesale hardware and DIY outlet.'

'Bobby' Giddens commented about Heffernan's brief stay in the English League, that 'Heff' made the mistake of 'parking his hat in a dressing-room of stars'. Greyhounds' line-up that year was: Jimmy Foster; Dick Adolph, Hazen McAndrew, 'Buck' Jones; 'Duke' Campbell, Joe Beaton, Earl Nicholson; Jake Brunning, Dunc Cheyne, Joe Shack; and 'Heff'.

Heffernan went on to be a big star in Canada, first for the 'amateur' Royals and then for Montreal Canadiens of the NHL, Les Habitants icing the 'Razzle-Dazzle' line in its entirety. He and I had plans to bring a group of Montreal stars to Britain for the first post-war season but we got the brush-off from Wembley, Nottingham and others, and Heffernan gave up his hockey interests to become a successful insurance broker, although he played veterans' hockey for many years.

Hogarth, his travelling companion and fellow-sufferer (only on Racers' bench), was not so lucky. Forgetting he was not in Canada he stepped off a kerb looking the wrong way and was taken to hospital after a car hit him.

Heffernan and his wife Kit now live in California and in December 1986 they met up with former Wembley forward 'Jo-Jo' Grabowski, who was visiting a daughter in San Rafael. Gerry told 'Jo-Jo' that I was writing the story of British ice hockey and the latter kindly recalled some of his memories of England.

Grabowski, whose defenceman brother Tony played for Hershey B'ars and then Montreal Canadiens, was himself rated Canada's top amateur at one time. Like Archie Stinchcombe, he had full sight in only one eye and Heffernan, who played against him when 'Jo-Jo' was with Quebec Aces and Valleyfield Braves, says: 'I must admit we were always told to come in on his blind side – but he was awfully fast.' Grabowski and Stinchcombe were not the only players so handicapped. Tommy Burlington, who had a successful career in professional ranks, had only one eye, and there have also been others.

After the Second World War English hockey had a referee, Bill Lewthwaite, who was similarly handicapped. Yet Bill was rated one of the film industry's top editors and, although no Ernie Leacock, he was not the world's worst referee either. His disability was never mentioned in *Ice Hockey World*. It is a cruel world out there and it was thought that some fans would never give Bill a moment's peace if they found out about his sight.

Grabowski confirms recollections of the financial situation. Most Wembley players received £10 weekly, plus £2 for a win, £1 for a draw. He paid only 22s. for his room and board.

Grabowski rates 'Lou' Bates as the best and most dramatic player ever to play in England. 'He could carry the puck through the opposition whenever he wished to do so — the fans loved him and fully recognised his great talent.' He also recalls the French-Canadian players who were switched from Paris to Manchester and Southampton when the franc was devalued as 'a happy and boisterous band'. They loved a good time, so Paris had been like Heaven to them. When they came to England it was necessary to make new financial arrangements, and Rapids, who had been taken under Harringay's wing, were interviewed individually by Percy Nicklin. Frankie Cadorette, later a popular Wembley player, emerged from the interview looking dazed. His team-mate, Larry Laframboise, asked how it went. Cadorette, whose spoken English was fractured to say the least, replied, 'He *axed* me to play for the glory.' No wonder the French-Canadians sometimes played as if their hearts were not in it!

Grabowski also recalls Wembley Lions' participation in the World Cup in Toronto, the other teams being Sudbury Frood (Allan Cup winners), Winnipeg Monarchs (Memorial Cup winners), and Hershey B'ars, from the United States. Sudbury won the round-robin tournament.

Grabowski thoroughly enjoyed his hockey in England, as did most of the players he has spoken with over the years.

The major talking point of the 1937—38 season was Claude Langdon's enterprise in arranging for top professional clubs, Montreal Canadiens and Detroit Red Wings, to play exhibition games at Empress Hall and Brighton as a climax to the season. Arguments raged as to whether or not an All Star team from the English League could hold its own against the professionals, but it was never put to the test as Canadiens and Wings were content to play each other. It could have been interesting, because of players in the English National League before the war thirty-six went on to play professional hockey, all but six of them playing in the NHL at some time or another.

In 1948, for example, professional hockey's *Who's Who* listed twenty players who had or would play in the English or Scottish National Leagues. They were: Gerry Brown (Earls Court Rangers), Fred Ferens (Wembley Monarchs), Tommy Forgie (Richmond Hawks, Brighton Tigers and Perth Panthers), Harvey Fraser (Wembley Monarchs), Gaston Gauthier (Harringay Greyhounds), 'Dutch' Hiller (Harringay Greyhounds), Alvin 'Buck' Jones (Harringay Greyhounds), Bob Kirkpatrick (Earls Court Royals), Leo Lamoureux (Earls Court Rangers), Tony Licari (Harringay Racers), Hazen McAndrew (Harringay Greyhounds), Johnny Mahaffy (Streatham), Jake Milford (Wembley Monarchs), George Pearson (Manchester Rapids and Harringay Racers), Joe Shack (Harringay Greyhounds and Racers), Gordon 'Moose' Sherritt (Harringay Greyhounds), Rene Trudell (Harringay Racers), Bobby Walton (Wembley Lions), Bob Whitelaw (Harringay Racers), and Bill Woodward (Streatham).

Ten years previously the touring teams boasted some of the great names of professional hockey. Canadiens had 'Toe' Blake, Stanley Cup winner as both player and coach; 'Black Cat' Johnny Gagnon; 'Silver Fox' Pit Lepine; Ti-Georges Mantha, and little Paul 'Polly' Drouin, an attack completed by Paul Haynes and Rod Lorrain. Welsh-born netman Wilf Cude had three big defenders in front of him in Walt Buswell, 'Babe' Siebert and 'Red' Goupille. Siebert, alas, was to drown in a boating accident in 1939.

Red Wings boasted even more great names, if that were possible. There was a brilliant goalie, Norm Smith, and hockey immortals such as Hec Kilrea, Modere 'Mud' Bruneteau, Syd Howe, Marty Barry, Eb Goodfellow, Doug Young, Eddie Wares, Carl Liscombe and Larry Aurie. With an eye to the box-office Wings also brought along as third defenceman the giant Pete Bessone, known to European fans because of a stint in Paris, a city to which he would one day return.

They were all top-class men; few bad hockey players ever broke into the exclusive club which was the NHL in those days.

The domestic National League continued to attract big crowds, but domination of the circuit moved across North London from Wembley to Harringay, Racers winning the Championship in 1938 and Greyhounds in 1939.

Ice hockey had all the glamour of show business in those days

Harringay Racers 1937–38, League Champions. Standing, left to right: Bob Whitelaw, Wilf Arnott, George Pearson, Percy Nicklin (coach), 'Lefty' Taylor (asst trainer), Major W.H. Mackenzie (manager), Bert Peer, Archie Creighton, Steve Latoski, 'Nobby' Clarke (trainer). Kneeling: Jack Keating, Andy Goldie, 'Fan' Heximer, Wally Monson, Len Burrage, Bill Hogarth.

Wembley Monarchs 1937–38, runners-up National League. Left to right: Clint Benedict (coach) (one of professional hockey's all-time great goalies), Alex Sinclair, Frankie Leblanc, Wally Rost, Rene Lortie, Sammy Gigliotti, Jake Milford, Len Godin, Jimmy Haggarty, Gordon Dailley and Jakie Nash (who was in the nets for the 1936 Canadian Olympic squad).

— live music, skating exhibitions by the world's best in the intervals, and the ice swept with military precision by a line of men in uniform, their brooms going backwards and forwards in time to martial music. Very often there would be famous names at rinkside — actors and actresses, top footballers, champion boxers — especially at Wembley where it was possible to eat dinner and watch the game at the same time.

In the seven-team League (Southampton and Manchester had gone and after two bitter experiences Earls Court iced only one team) the 1937–38 Racers, perhaps the best-balanced side ever seen in Great Britain, finished thirteen points ahead of Lions and Monarchs, fourteen ahead of their stable-mates Greyhounds. The team which achieved this overwhelming victory was: Andy Goldie; Len Burrage, Bob Whitelaw, George Pearson; Bert Peer, Wally Monson, 'Fan' Heximer; Archie Creighton, Steve Latoski, Jack Keating; Billy Hogarth. Latoski was the League's leading scorer.

Greyhounds were champions the following season with Foster still in goal, Hazen McAndrew, Dick 'Dutch' Behling and Connie Tudin on defence, Duke Campbell, Joe Beaton and 'Fan' Heximer, one line, and Jake Brunning, Dunc Cheyne and Joe Shack, the other, the famous 'Kid Line'. Centre Bill McGregor was the spare forward.

Internationally, Great Britain retained the European Championship in 1938 by virtue of beating Czechoslovakia in the final pool. Unfortunately they lost 3–1 to Canada and so missed a good chance of regaining the World title, since the Sudbury team which represented Canada bore no resemblance to the squad which won the Allan Cup in 1937. Foster, Davey, Dailley, Archer, Stinchcombe, Chappell and Kelly shouldered the British burden, but it was encouraging for the future of ice hockey that six home-bred players were included: Reg Merrifield, the Sussex goalie; Woolsley (Earls Court Redwings), Ridley (Earls Court Marlboroughs), Willson (Earls Court Redwings), Halford (Queens) and Wyman (Queens) who, of course, had been on the Olympic team.

The following season the European title went to Switzerland. Foster, Kelly and Dailley were the only National League players in the British line-up and this time the load was too much. Team selection aroused great controversy. It was rumoured that Nicklin had little say in choosing his squad, being asked only to eliminate three from a final choice of sixteen put before him. Indeed, it was said he had to fight to get Kelly on the team. But the BIHA wanted to encourage home-bred players and 'Bunny' Ahearne replied to criticism with 'Hell, can't we take a licking.'

Against a great team like Trail Smoke Eaters we had to! Smoke Eaters added lustre to the season when they toured England and Scotland after the Championships, and there were other milestones along the way: Wembley experimented with a *red* puck; Blackpool saw ice hockey for the first time in December 1937, when London Canadians, led by Blane Sexton, beat Queens, captained by 'Doc' Kellough, 6–4.

Wembley formed a Junior League in 1937–38 with four teams, Cubs, Wolves, Princes and Panthers, a league which eventually produced some National League-calibre players. Harringay followed suit in 1938–39.

The London-Provincial League of that season had twelve teams and might well have developed some good home talent had not war intervened. The teams involved were Oxford and Cambridge Universities, Cambridge Grads, Earls Court Red-wings and Marlboroughs, United Hospitals, Sussex, Princes, Bournemouth, Queens, Streatham Royals and Wembley Terriers.

The major headlines in the last peacetime season for seven years were reserved, unfortunately, for the saddest and sorriest episode in the history of the sport in this country, an episode which did little credit to any of the parties involved.

At the centre of the affair was the League team with the longest tradition, Streatham. It is undeniable that in the 1938–39 season they had three or four players with quick tempers, not least their French-Canadian goalminder, Louis St Denis. St Denis was an experienced veteran of the hockey wars — he toured Europe with the 1935 Ottawa team — and his actions were hard to explain. He was sent off against Earls Court Rangers and against Harringay Racers for throwing his stick at the opposition. In the Harringay game, another fiery player, centreman 'Toots' Day guarded the nets whilst St Denis was in the penalty-box for one minute. Racers scored — and Day came rushing out to protest, jostling referee Ernie Leacock in the process.

In a match between Wembley Monarchs and Streatham two players of good reputation, Frankie Cadorette and Bill Wood-ward, fought. It might not have amounted to much had not a steward joined in, throwing a punch at Woodward. Dailley and Lortie joined in for Monarchs, and Day, Tomalty and Bean came in to help their team-mate.

Day was involved in another incident in a so-called 'friendly' between Wembley All Stars and Streatham, although to be fair to him he only lost his temper after the normally sensible Gordon Dailley crashed Henry Hayes, Roland Reeves and Day himself into the boards in quick succession.

Back at Harringay St Denis went into the penalty-box for the third time (a record for a British goalie), on this occasion for slashing at Jake Brunning. Day was acting up again and Jules Blais tried to get at the referee. It was contagious. Greyhound defenceman Hazen McAndrew suddenly exploded and felled the unsuspecting Roland Reeves, who had to be carried off.

The upshot of this behaviour was that St Denis, Day and Blais were all handed suspensions by the BIHA. Streatham asked for the suspensions to be deferred since Reeves, Hayes and Bobby Beaton were all on the injured list, leaving them with only five senior players. The BIHA turned them down, and it is perhaps unfortunate that at this crucial time Secretary 'Bunny' Ahearne was engaged on ice hockey affairs in Europe. Had he been about, the BIHA might have taken a more lenient attitude.

Despite their request being turned down, Streatham iced all three suspended men against Brighton, defeating the Tigers 5–4. The Streatham management said it was the only way they could keep faith with the public. The quarrel with the BIHA assumed greater proportions and while the row was still going on Streatham played Monarchs, winning 3–2 despite icing junior coach Ernie 'Al' Batson and one of his players, Pete Ravenscroft. In fact, Batson in particular did well. It was a very rough game, however, perhaps not surprisingly in view of what had happened in earlier encounters between the two teams, and when Woodward was penalised by referee Hank Wilson, he assaulted the luckless official.

It was all very sad. Streatham were expelled from the League and Woodward suspended for two years. A clean-cut youngster and a very good winger, Woodward was qualified by birth for England and had been chosen by the BIHA for several representative matches, but there is little doubt that he, like several of his team-mates, the Streatham management and many of their supporters, developed a persecution complex during the latter part of the season. Most of the other Streatham players were suspended, the periods varying from the remainder of the season to the end of the following season. The exceptions were Beaton, Hayes and Reeves, all injured at the relevant times, and the innocent Batson and Ravenscroft. Batson, who later played and coached (very successfully) in Scotland, was an interesting character who might have had a more illustrious hockey career had he not been bitten by the stage bug, touring as a big band singer under the name 'Al Batson'. Six feet one inch and weighing 210lb, he too was qualified for Great Britain.

There were many great games during the Golden Age of hockey, but if one had to choose a single night to remember it could well be 12 November 1938 when Earls Court Rangers journeyed to Harringay to play Greyhounds.

The 'Blues' boasted such hockey immortals as Jimmy Foster, Duke Campbell and Joe Beaton; the original 'Kid Line' of Dunc Cheyne, Jake Brunning and Joe Shack; not one but three defencemen who would turn professional – Dick 'Dutch' Behling, Hazen McAndrew and Connie Tudin; and a blond youngster labelled as Canada's best amateur the previous season, Jack Atchison (not to be confused with Johnny Acheson who earned the same label).

This then was the power-house confronting Rangers in a National Tournament game on a cold and wintry night.

The gate in the barrier opened and Rangers took the ice. Frail, white-faced goaler Harry Braithwaite, jumpy and excited because he was battling for his job with a player named Gib Hutchinson; rough and tough Frank Currie, the 'Blond Bombshell' they called him then, who was to lead Edmonton Flyers to the Allan Cup in 1948; Ab 'Two Ton' Tonn, likeable defence rookie whose big weakness was increasing weight and a yen for candy; Gerry Brown, Jack Forsey, Bill Jennings, Roland Reeves. Seven men — and the crowd waited expectantly for the remainder of the visiting team. There were no more, however. Bobby Lee, Leo Lamoureux, Bill Parsons and Howie Peterson were on the injured list, and even Currie and Reeves were playing against doctor's orders.

It looked like a Roman holiday for Greyhounds, but that gallant seven had other ideas. Jack Forsey was here, there and everywhere, a constant thorn in the Harringay defence. Gerry Brown backchecked like a madman, skated himself into the ice and could barely drag himself back to the bench when his all too infrequent rest periods came around.

Still Greyhounds smiled, confident that victory would be theirs.

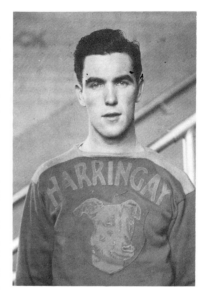

Then Roland Reeves scored on a Forsey assist. A minute later Gerry Brown added another. Joe Beaton reduced the arrears and then in the second period Rangers went wild — Forsey, Tonn and Forsey again blasting pucks past Foster. It was getting tougher and tougher for the outnumbered Rangers, and fast-breaking Tudin scored two in a row. But Forsey came back to complete a valiant hat trick.

The crowd was in uproar as Joe Beaton scored a fourth for Greyhounds, who were swarming around the Earls Court nets. Rangers were sold out and looked it. Then a careless pass went astray and Bill Jennings, Rangers' fastest forward, was the man who intercepted it. Every one of the home team, bar goalie Foster, was trapped in the wrong end — and Jennings made no mistake.

The seven cripples had achieved the impossible. They had taken Greyhounds 7–4, and the measure of their achievement was that Greyhounds went on to win the National League for the first time. Even the most ardent Harringay fan could scarce forbear to cheer that magnificent seven in the orange-and-chocolate of Rangers.

Three powerful defencemen who played a major role in Harringay Greyhounds winning the League championship in 1939 – Dick Behling (opposite), Hazen McAndrew (top) and Connie Tudin (bottom). With the legendary Foster behind them, 'Hounds had the lowest goals against in the circuit.'

7 AFTER THE SIREN SOUNDED

Berlin, bombed and in ruins – two men in British Army 'warms' pick their way through the debris which was once the headquarters of the Third Reich, Hitler's Chancellery. 'We're a long way from Wembley,' muses one. 'Perhaps now we'll soon be back,' replied the other.

Hundreds of miles from the Empire Pool & Sports Arena, Major Gordon Dailley, of Grosvenor House Canadians, Wembley Canadians, Wembley Monarchs, Wembley Lions and the Great Britain Championship team of 1936, had met up with Captain Ian Gordon, ice hockey correspondent of the *Daily Graphic*.

They were not the first ice hockey folk into Berlin. That honour went to another Wembley defenceman and British international, Jimmy Carr, officer commanding a Field Squadron of the Royal Engineers. Nor was that the end of the tale. Ian Gordon was at Brigade Headquarters one day when a German in civilian clothes presented himself and asked if there were any jobs going. His face looked familiar to Ian. 'Aren't you Rudi Ball?' he asked; and it was.

Rudi Ball was Germany's greatest ice hockey player, but he had Jewish blood and was frowned upon by Hitler and his henchmen. However, the glory of the Third Reich was more important than their hatred of Jews, and Ball was restored to favour to lead the German team in the 1936 Olympics.

Now Ball had survived the war and here he was asking the British Army for a job. Despite what is often said about the military, on this occasion they found a square hole for a square peg. Ball was put in charge of an open-air ice rink and thousands of servicemen learned to skate there. It was one little happy ending to a story that had begun six years before.

Within minutes of Prime Minister Neville Chamberlain's announcement that Britain was at war with Germany, the air raid warning sirens sounded in London. It was a false alarm and the six months 'phoney war' which followed gave an unexpected and welcome but temporary reprieve to organised League hockey. Both in Scotland and England plans were made for emergency competitions, pooling player resources where necessary.

Some players destined for British clubs had not left Canada when war broke out and around thirty others, already in Britain, left for home, at least one contingent having a U-boat scare on the way; others were on the Athenia which was torpedoed. Those players who left could hardly be blamed. Many of them had wives and families in Canada and the future here looked very uncertain. Fortunately, many others decided to stay and see what happened.

Scotland had been planning the biggest season yet and some high-class talent had been recruited. Six rinks wanted to stage first-class hockey – Ayr, Dundee, Dunfermline, Falkirk, Kirkcaldy and Perth – and when the SIHA counted heads they found they had around fifty puck-chasers, Canadian and Scottish, of senior calibre.

It was decided that each rink could claim four 'regulars' and the rest of the players would be pooled and divided up. On paper at least, the teams seemed evenly balanced. Dundee had goalie Bill Lane, former Earls Court defencemen George McNeil and Merrick Cranstoun, Al Rogers, ex-Brighton winger, 'Scotty' Cameron and Laurie Marchant amongst their allocation.

Dunfermline had 'Chick' Kerr in the nets, 'Red' Thomson, Tommy Durling (ex-Streatham), Jimmy Chappell and Norman McQuade. Kirkcaldy's goalie was Art Grant with Les Lovell and George Horne on the blue-line, Glenn Morrison, Arnie Pratt, Frank Chase and Jimmy Shannon up-front.

'Scottie' Milne was back in the Perth nets, and Panthers also had Les Tapp (who had married Pat Burgess in London) 'Bunt' Roberts, Art Schumann, 'Breezy' Thompson, Tommy McInroy and Jimmy Allan.

Falkirk had Scots goalie Willie Turnbull, the Beaton brothers Bobby and Clem, Alex Purdie, Gerry Davey, Bill Bodnar and George McWilliams, while Ayr lined-up with 'Buster' Amantea, Art Shires, Cummine, Cumming, Welsh, McAlpine, McLeod and fast-skating Richmond and Harringay winger, Earl 'Sparky' Nicholson.

Once the season got under way changes had to be made, but at least the Scottish authorities had approached the problem sensibly and logically.

Ayr lost Nicholson, who had a good offer from a Canadian club and decided to go home. Kirkcaldy signed dapper Wembley centreman Paul Rheault who was to prove one of the top stars of the season, masterminding a line with big Arnie Pratt and little Glenn Morrison on his wings.

Streatham's ace goalie, big Maurice Gerth, had signed for

Falkirk before war was declared. He arrived back in London to marry his sweetheart, played for a month with Wembley Lions, then headed north to take up position between the Falkirk pipes.

Many of the players in Scotland found war jobs to do when they were not playing. A number of them were working in the fields near Rosyth when the air raid warnings sounded. 'There was no panic but we ran like hell,' reported Jimmy Chappell.

The Scottish decision to go ahead was a success from the start. Perth and Ayr were soon getting capacity crowds and full houses followed at most of the rinks. Perth Panthers emerged as Champions of the Scottish War Emergency League Points Tournament, and Dunfermline Vikings took the Scottish Cup after no less than two play-off series with Falkirk Lions, Vikings winning the final game 4–3 after three overtime periods.

South of the Border hockey was saved by a contingent of puck-chasers from Manitoba who had been recruited by Percy Nicklin for the two Harringay clubs. They were offered jobs in a factory run by Harringay general manager, Major W.H. Mackenzie and, with one exception, they all agreed to stay. Harringay sportingly offered to loan some of them out to other teams if it would help the English National League to be run.

There were other difficulties apart from player shortage. Although Harringay had spent a lot of money on black-out material, they were told that matches would have to be played in the afternoon and that attendance would be restricted to 4,000 spectators. Four thousand duly turned up for the first match of the season on 7 October, played between Racers and Greyhounds.

Referees were in short supply, ex professional Dinn Lecrook being about the only experienced referee available. For a while *Ice Hockey World* editor, 'Bobby' Giddens, was pressed into service. He was a good editor but a bad referee.

Harringay's goodwill overflowed into the BIHA offices where it was decided to advise the Canadian authorities that the ban imposed on Streatham players Bill Woodward, Louis St Denis and Gordon 'Toots' Day the previous season would be lifted. The BIHA and SIHA, who had been in dispute over Scotland's claim for self-determination, also signed a peace treaty, the British art of compromise satisfying both sides, more or less.

A four-team London Cup – Harringay Racers and Greyhounds, Wembley Lions and Streatham – launched English competition. Brighton, left out through shortage of players and wartime travel difficulties, promptly organised the Sussex Ice Hockey League with all-local talent making up four teams. Such

Nottingham Ice Stadium, which opened for hockey in the first wartime season was designed as a scaled-down version of Harringay Arena.

British born-and-bred players came into their own in wartime hockey. Some of the most successful ones are seen practising at Wembley: Doug Young, Johnny Murray, Johnny Oxley and Maurice 'Stan' Simon.

was the enthusiasm for hockey in the seaside town that crowds of 2,500 turned out to watch these matches. Nottingham was also left out of contention but Nottingham Panthers still made their début in the new Stadium, losing 7−4 to the Canadians of RAF (Grantham). That first Panther squad, now mostly forgotten, was: Torgalson; Spencer, J. Block, R. Block, Brown, Rivett, Lee, Max Keller, White, Jones and Raines.

Racers won the London Cup with Englishman Maurice 'Stan' Simon in the nets and two other English players, Tommy Grace and 'Pip' Perrin. Former right-winger Archie Creighton turned out to be a good defender and they had veteran centreman

Archie Creighton, veteran forward of Winnipeg Monarchs and Harringay Racers converted to defence with great success in wartime hockey.

Wally 'Pop' Monson to steady five of the Canadian newcomers, Doug Rose, Tommy Wheeler, Bill Klem, Rene Trudell and Lindsay McDougall. It was the dash of Trudell and McDougall, added to the wiles of the 'Old Fox' Monson, that made Racers' first line the best in the competition.

With a group of itinerant puck-chasers surfacing in London, Wembley decided to revive Monarchs to make a five-team National League. On their first appearance Monarchs had wandering Al McKendrick, a merchant seaman who had previously done duty as spare goalie with Fife Flyers, Cam Shewan, hard-hitting Lions rearguard, and very experienced forwards like Brighton's Jimmy Kelly, the much-travelled Frankie Green and Hymie McArthur, and speedy left-winger 'Fan' Heximer from Harringay. Ace Harringay defenceman Bob McCranor was switched to Streatham as player-coach, and the League got under way.

Earl's Court were showing interest and recalled the veteran George Strubbe to look after hockey activities. It did not prove possible to ice a League team but, with the Canadian forces in Britain in large numbers, the Empress Hall became headquarters for a number of their teams.

The first Canadian Army opposition was seen at Harringay on 16 January 1940 when Greyhounds defeated the Horse Artillery 8–5, but before that two Wembley junior teams, the Terriers and Colts, played the first ice hockey match on Irish soil in December at King's Hall, Balmoral, Belfast.

For the rest of the season, service teams figured prominently at all the southern rinks. Former Earls Court Ranger defenceman Harry Brown was on one of the Army teams, and there were some useful puck-chasers around. Services hockey was welcomed by both the Canadian authorities and the British Government, and in March Winston Churchill and Anthony Eden were at Wembley to see the Royal Canadian Artillery (2nd Regiment) defeat Toronto Scottish 7–2. The two statesmen insisted on being introduced to the teams.

Brighton changed the name of their local league from Sussex to Brighton and from the pick of the four sides formed Sussex Tigers, with British international Reg Merriefield in goal and four or five Canadians including Haines, who had been destined for Earls Court Rangers if war had not intervened. The star of the Sussex side was the 'pride of Scotland', Billy Fullerton, now a flier in the RAF.

The domestic League, with the teams at last sorted out reasonably well, was exciting, with Harringay Greyhounds pipping Racers by one point despite the loss of McCranor. The

Championship team was: Len Kennedy; Gordon Sherritt and Bob Wyman; Joe Beaton, Dunc Cheyne and 'Duke' Campbell; Tommy Wheeler, Freddie Dunkelman and Art Ridley. Ray Neilson, Nigel Fitch and Percy Eves also played, the winning team thus including five men who, but for the emergency, might have been playing for non-League teams.

Greyhounds also took the National Tournament, and such was the optimism after a good season that Harringay even planned to send Percy Nicklin on a scouting trip to Canada to secure players for the 1940–41 season. Before that could happen the much-vaunted Maginot Line had collapsed before the German hordes, the remnants of the British Army had escaped via Dunkirk and the war was on in earnest. Hockey had to take a back seat.

The light was not extinguished completely, however. Hockey continued to be played in a number of rinks scattered over the United Kingdom. In Scotland, stars such as Rheault, McNeil and Cameron were active. Juniors were encouraged, and Cameron's work with the youngsters was rewarded in 1945–46 when Dunfermline Royals won the Scottish Junior League. The Royals had two big defencemen, 'Tiny' and 'Tuck' Syme, from tough Fifeshire mining stock, who would make quite a name for themselves after the war.

In March 1940 the Durham rink opened, brain-child of Alderman 'Icy' Smith, twice Mayor of Darlington and a most remarkable character. He too founded a hockey dynasty with sons and grandsons lacing their boots in the Durham dressing-rooms. The rink was at first a makeshift arrangement with a marquee roof supported by poles to keep the elements at bay. Yet during the war years it witnessed matches in which some of the world's greatest players appeared, amongst them Boston Bruins' immortal 'Kraut Line' of Milt Schmidt, Bobby Bauer and 'Woody' Dumart.

Talking of Dumart, he is a classic example of the difficulties sports historians face in getting names and nicknames correct. In Boston's *Who's Who* he is listed as 'Woodrow Clarence (Porky) Dumart'. In the NHL's similar publication, he appears as 'Woodrow Wilson Dumart'. With a choice between a dead US President, a name like Clarence and a nickname such as 'Porky', it is little wonder that Dumart preferred to be known as 'Woody'.

'Icy' Smith was the king of everything he surveyed. Some time after the war ended – when Durham Wasps were carrying all before them outside senior league ranks – BIHA Secretary 'Bunny' Ahearne asked me to accompany 'Bibo' de Marwicz,

Three boys from Portage La Prairie Terriers who helped to keep hockey going in 1939–40: René Trudell (opposite, below), Len Kennedy (top) and Lindsay McDougall (bottom).

former Streatham and England player, to Durham to run the
rule over the Wasps and see which of them were likely candidates for the British World Championship team. In the middle
of a period we were startled to hear a stentorian voice bellow,
'Referee, send off that Number Three.' 'Icy' had decided that
one of the opposition was being unkind to his beloved Wasps so
he grabbed the rinkside microphone from his startled
announcer and ordered the referee to take action.

On another occasion 'Icy' and I went to Whitley Bay so that
he could show me where he was going to build a new rink. We
drove down the promenade in the middle of the road at about
fifteen miles per hour with a procession, including a police car,
building up behind us. Hesitantly I suggested that we pull over.
'Nonsense,' said 'Icy', 'they all know me here.' Fair enough, but
when he took both hands off the wheel to demonstrate a point, I
prayed that our guardian angel also knew him well.

British hockey, both in Scotland and England, owes a lot to
'Icy'. His memorials are not so much the rinks he left behind
him but the teams – Durham Wasps, Whitley Warriors and
Cleveland Bombers; and who knows if Crowtree Chiefs would
ever have seen the light of day had it not been for the inspiration
of 'Icy'.

With the end of the war in Europe ice hockey became more
general, but the cost had been high. Scotland's finest home-
grown player, Billy Fullerton, had been killed in action, and so
too had Kirkcaldy goalminder Art Grant, Jackie Johnston and
Jock Taylor, of Falkirk, and Scottish junior, Flt.Lt. Frankie
Banner, whose father subsequently donated the Banner Trophy
in his son's memory. Brighton, Wembley and Great Britain
centreman, Jimmy Kelly, was killed in Holland; the colourful
and controversial 'Toots' Day in action with the RCAF. Two
Earls Court players died in action: Maule Colledge, brother of
world skating champion, Cecilia; and Bill Parsons, Rangers'
Canadian defenceman.

Others had gone too. Harringay trainer Nobby Clarke died
after a long illness; Wembley centre Frankie Leblanc was killed
in a hunting accident; and Roy Musgrove, one of Wembley's
greatest goalies, who was a highly qualified engineer, died in a
mining accident in Flin-Flon.

The Canadian services still provided the life-blood of British
hockey. Official Services Championships were held at Durham,
Ayr and Paisley in 1945 and at Wembley and Brighton in 1946.

In Scotland, where there had been more wartime hockey than in the south, everyone was very enthusiastic. Down south, although Brighton had staged hockey every Sunday throughout the war and Purley too had been active, it took the reopening of Wembley to give the sport a much-needed shot in the arm.

1945–46 was an amazing season considering the world situation. Sweden and Switzerland, two neutral nations, visited Britain but so, surprisingly, did Czechoslovakia.

RCAF Meteors won the Canadian Services Hockey League, Hurricanes the RCAF Championship, and Maple Leafs the Army title. All three teams were packed with professional and senior amateur players like high-scoring Hub Macey (New York Rangers), Bud Poile (Toronto Maple Leafs), Jack Giesbrecht (Detroit Red Wings), Pete Langelle (Toronto Maple Leafs), Eddie Bush (Detroit Red Wings), Johnnie Mowers (Detroit Red Wings) and 'Turk' Broda (Toronto Maple Leafs).

Broda, despite his reputation, could be a disappointing man to watch at times. The first time I saw him in action at Brighton he was beaten six times, and Gib Hutchinson in the opposing nets looked a much safer bet. A wiser head than mine pointed out that the 'Turk', one of the game's greatest shut-out kings, was a money player: 'See him in the Stanley Cup play-offs and you won't recognise him as the same guy.' It was a fact that Broda, who tended to tubbiness, had to have the Riot Act read to him at one stage of his illustrious career with Toronto; he was definitely a man for the big occasion.

Pete Langelle hit the headlines for reasons other than his not

The first post-war Lions, standing, left to right: Archie Stinchcombe, 'Sonny' Rost, Johnny Oxley, 'Lou' Bates, Arthur Green, Bob Wyman, Freddie Sutherland; kneeling: Pete Smith, Gib Hutchinson, Joe Beaton.

inconsiderable hockey ability. He was one of the pilots credited with shooting-up a car in which a German Field Marshal was travelling. At the time it was believed to be Germany's best soldier, Erwin Rommel.

Big Eddie Bush was an NHL 'badman', but in 1945–46 he was made to look almost angelic by a mustachiod right-winger from the Canadian Army named Freddie Sutherland. Sutherland would stay in England to become a regular with Wembley and Brighton. After he retired he opened a restaurant in Sussex where he still lives, one of a considerable contingent of players, both pre- and post-war, who settled down in that area.

One of them, Denis Hammond, former Sussex player and *Ice Hockey World* sub-editor, has made several abortive attempts to get a new ice stadium off the ground in that region, notably at Portsmouth. Wembley defenceman Roy Shepherd is another who has kept trying. As this book is written it seems that constant dripping may have worn away the stone and a new rink for Brighton is a distinct possibility.

Other 1945–46 stars included pre-war English League players like Bobby Lee, Joe Beaton, Archie Stinchcombe, Jimmy Haggarty, Alex Archer, Bob Whitelaw, 'Sonny' Rost, 'Duke' Campbell and Frankie Green, and two of the best-ever British born-and-bred players, Johnny Oxley and Arthur Green.

There were others in addition to Sutherland who would return in post-war hockey, notably Tony Licari and Frankie Boucher.

The first post Second World War Lions, who did battle with the services and overseas clubs, were: Gib Hutchinson (goal); Lou Bates, Sonny Rost and Bob Wyman (defence); Johnnie Oxley, Freddie Sutherland and Pete Smith, who were to become known as 'The SOS Line'; and Joe Beaton, Archie Stinchcombe and Arthur Green.

Brighton, not to be left out, staged a Victory Tournament between teams representing Brighton, Wembley and Earls Court, and with fine players, packed houses and post-war euphoria, British hockey was all set for another Golden Era which would last through to the mid-1950s.

The world's first ice hockey newspaper, *Ice Hockey World*, was all set to return, and the rebirth of weekly publication was heralded by some pocket magazines which are now collectors' items. Believe it or not, the Editor and Assistant Editor, Giddens and myself, sold these magazines from a kiosk in the Wembley concourse. Sir Arthur Elvin gave us an empty kiosk rent-free providing we had the guts to sell our own publication. We did – and he kept his word.

8 DROPPING THE PUCK

They were fresh off the boat from Canada. England in that harsh, cold and snowy winter of 1947 did not look so very different from back home in Regina. 'Stubby' Mason and George Beach had come over to play hockey at Wembley. They had been warned that the country was still in bad shape after the war and there was still not much to eat because of food rationing, so they were a bit surprised when they sat down for their first meal in England at the Empire Pool and were given heaped-up plates. Stubby took a bite, swallowed and then asked the waiter what it was. Proudly he said that the chef had made a 'special' for them and it was called 'Toad in the Hole'. Stubby immediately choked and George went white.

Later George related: 'We knew things were rough, but not that tough. We really believed that the country was down to eating toads. Needless to say we were calmed down and told it was merely sausage in a batter. It was one experience I've never forgotten.'

Beach made England his home from that day to this, although making frequent trips back to Canada. He was to play with Wembley Monarchs and Lions and later with the Wembley

Stubby Mason, Wembley and Fife goalminder and great character, draws a lucky number for a spectator at a charity match. Alan Weeks, then Brighton Publicity Manager, is at the microphone.

George Beach (Wembley Lions) is introduced to HRH The Duke of Edinburgh on the occasion of 'the Royal Command' match between Lions and All Stars. 'Bunny' Ahearne is the other man in the picture.

team that expired in 1969, having run out of feasible opposition. A centreman who rarely got a penalty, Beach, along with 'Chick' Zamick of Nottingham and Wembley, was one of only two players to score more than 1,000 goals in British ice hockey. His battle honours include: League Player of the Year; three times winner of Sir Noel Curtis Bennett Sportsman's Bowl; League All Star centre; winner of Autumn Cup, International Trophy and National League scoring championships; and winner of Autumn Cup, International Trophy and National League Championship medals. When his playing career finished, he coached and managed Great Britain in the World Championships in Poland, and for the first time a British team won the Fair Play Trophy. 'Bunny' Ahearne was delighted.

George recalls how the weather affected hockey in those days when fog was commonplace in the winter months. 'There were those pea-soupers we used to have when we had to take it in turns to walk to Brighton in front of the bus and then skate around the ice with blankets to try and clear the fog in the rink. After the game we had to turn round and walk back to London in front of the bus, carrying a torch so that the driver could follow us. One night when Brighton Tigers were playing at Wembley, over 2,000 people had to stay the night in the ice rink because the fog was so bad.'

Mason, alas, is no longer alive. On his day he was a great goalminder, but sometimes temperament got the better of him. Sports folk have long contended that all goalies are mad, in football, field and ice hockey; 'Stubby' was probably a little

Some of Kewley's 'Army'. A group of puck-chasers bound for the Scottish League arrive at Liverpool and are met by Nelson McCuaig, Falkirk coach (left), Bob Giddens and Phil Drackett, *Ice Hockey World* (centre), and Frank Chase, Ayr coach (right). Most of these players, including Gibson, Clancy, Burns, Evans, Finch and Leadbeater, stayed to be stars in Scotland.

more eccentric than most. On one trip to Nottingham he took a dislike to some of the hotel furniture and promptly got rid of it – out of the window. That cost the Wembley management a few pounds.

In his second season, however, he headed the goalminders' averages all year and was one of the main reasons Monarchs won both the National Tournament and the International Trophy. He played for Fife Flyers after leaving Wembley.

The Scots were the first to get under way with competitive hockey after the war, Falkirk, Dundee, Kirkcaldy, Ayr, Paisley, Perth and Dunfermline all being ready for action. Toronto newsman Claude Kewley was recruited to scout players for the Scottish League, the idea being that if one man, applying the same standards of judgement, selected all the players, they could be divided amongst the teams in such a way as to give fair and balanced line-ups and hopefully close competition. It was a task in which Kewley would be succeeded by his son Keith.

There were seventy young Canadians in Kewley's first selection, among them two of his six sons, Herb, who became one of the better defencemen in the League, and the aforementioned Keith, who turned his hand to coaching. Some of that first band were to become great names in British hockey, notably defenceman Art Hodgins, now living in retirement in the Midlands after an illustrious career in both Scotland and England.

Scottish fans were hungry for League hockey and spectators were turned away from a packed Dunfermline rink as the local Vikings trounced Falkirk Lions 9–2, plump Joe 'Krumpy' Kromptich scoring six.

On the whole, the idea of Kewley's 'Army' worked well, but inevitably not all the seventy players came up to scratch and some teams came out of the deal better than others. Also, ten players per team gave no margin for injuries, so a reserve pool of 'old timers' was formed: Dave Cross, Laurie Marchant, Alex Purdie, Jimmy Allan, Don Cumming, Dave Logan, Jimmy Shannon and Tommy Lauder. Marchant later became coach of Perth, Lauder of Paisley, while Cross was soon in action deputising for Falkirk's injured O'Connell. Reserve pool not-withstanding, Scotland later found it necessary to fly in three more players from Canada.

There was one other repercussion from a brave and enterprising experiment when in November Scotland's Canadians demanded £3 increase on their contracted £7 per week. For a while it seemed the League would have a strike on its hands, but the players eventually settled for an increase of £2.10s. per week, payable in a lump sum at the end of the season to every player completing his contract on a satisfactory basis.

Dunfermline Vikings were Scotland's Team of the Year, winning the League and the Canada Cup and being runners-up in the National Tournament. Managed by Scottish League veteran 'Scotty' Cameron and including the two Kewley brothers, Vikings had the top points- and goal-scorer in Johnny Myke, the defenceman giving most assists in Joe Lay and the

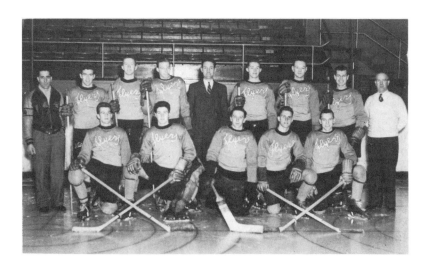

Fife Flyers 1946–47. Standing: Al Rogers (coach), Floyd Snider, Frank King, Jim McKenzie, Jack Wake (manager), Earl McCrone, Bob Londry, Pat Ratchford, James Forrest (trainer); kneeling: Bud Scrutton, John Drummond, Don Dougall, Bob Lantz, Harry O'Connor.

goalminder with the best defensive record in Ivan Walmsley.

Not only were Vikings the least scored upon team through the season but they were also the highest-scoring squad with 300 goals over all the tournaments. Perhaps surprisingly, only Walmsley and Lay were named All Stars. Walmsley and Harringay's Ed Blondin later played with Johnstown Jets when they won the US Senior Open Championship.

For those with the future of the game at heart perhaps the most encouraging aspect of the season was the keen competition in junior ranks, where Glasgow Mohawks won the Mitchell Cup and Banner Trophy and Kirkcaldy Juniors won the Frame and McPherson Trophies.

In England Wembley opened the season with a three-game series, Lions versus The Rest. True competition got under way with the Autumn Cup, a four team tournament comprising Brighton, Streatham and the two Wembley clubs. 'Red' Stapleford brought back many old favourites to Streatham, including Archie Stinchcombe, Frank Trottier, Gerry Davey, 'Chuck' Turner, Freddie Dunkelman and Maurice 'Stan' Simon. It was almost as if the war had never been.

October saw twenty-one players arrive bound for Harringay, and 'Lou' Bates brought over nine Canadians as reinforcements for Wembley. Meanwhile, 'Sandy' Archer left for Canada to recruit players for Nottingham.

Later the same month 'Mr Ice Hockey' of Paris, Charlie Michaelis, had a narrow escape when he was turned off a plane to make way for a VIP. The plane crashed on take-off and a number of passengers were killed.

Junior hockey in progress at Kirkcaldy.

Not so lucky were five members of the Czech team due to play in Great Britain who disappeared over the Channel in a hired aircraft. I will never forget that long, miserable wait in a London hotel with those of the team who were already here, waiting – and wondering. Some newspapers put forward the theory that the Czechs had defected, but if so no one has seen or heard of them to this day.

Another hockey player who died in somewhat similar circumstances a few years later was veteran goalminder of Earls Court Marlboroughs, 'Jock' Robin. 'Jock' was also a keen motor-racing man (like Streatham's Richard Bacon in more recent years) and was *en route* to the Le Mans 24-Hour Race when his plane nosedived into the Channel.

It is difficult in these days of jet aircraft, high-speed passenger trains and fast cars to appreciate the hazards and difficulties confronting touring teams in the years just after the Second World War. 'Duke' Campbell and I took a Harringay squad on a tour of Czechoslovakia in 1949 – difficult enough in all conscience, the Communists having not long taken over the country – and *en route* we had to land in Brussels because there was fog, snow and ice in Prague. On the way back we had to return to Prague when one of the engines failed. The pilot said the weather was bad over London, but Lorne Lussier and I at a window seat located over the engine with a stationary prop knew better.

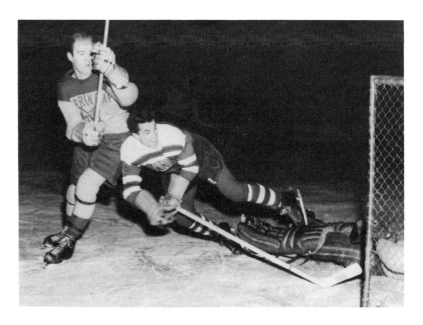

Defenceman Pat Coburn and goalie Lorne Lussier fail to prevent a goal during Racers' tour of Czechoslovakia.

It was with mixed feelings that we viewed ambulances and fire engines scooting around Prague airport as we prepared to land. Nothing, however, to the feelings of my bride of six months, waiting with Duke Macdonald at London's Kensington Air Terminal. With the flight some hours overdue they were told by a counter clerk, 'Last we heard they'd got engine trouble'.

As for the plane we used in Czechoslovakia ... We had played in Bratislava the night before and the Mayor, who kept a good line in Scotch, decided to give us a ceremonial send-off by marching us to the airfield (and it was a field) with a brass band at our head. I can still see that silver Douglas DC gleaming in the weak morning sun. We marched up to it – and round it. On the other side was one of those old 'corrugated iron' Fokkers, used in the war as a German troop-carrier.

George Steele, a Wembley Monarch before he joined Racers, was a nervous air passenger anyway; now he thought he spotted a leak from one of the engines and he rushed off to find the pilot, a Czech who had served in the RAF during the war. 'Not to worry,' said he, 'this is a fine aircraft. We used to have two of them.' 'What do you mean, *used* to have two?' asked the suspicious George. 'The other one crashed last week,' came the reply.

The Pope is not the first man to kiss the ground when alighting from an aircraft. Even Joe 'Iron Stomach' Shack, smoker of the foulest cigars ever, kissed the ground after our bumpy flight over the mountains to Ostrava.

Even more than in Scotland, improvisation was the order of the day in England during the immediate post-war period. Army Captain Gordie Poirier, whose professional career with Montreal Canadiens had been halted by the war, returned to Brighton with four-year-old son, Mike. Streatham recruited hard-working George Baillie from Scotland. Wembley released Gib Hutchinson to Brighton after it was pointed out that he and Bobby Lee, both under contract to Earls Court, had been offered to Tigers and no one else. Wembley's action cost British born-and-bred netman, 'Nobby' Richardson, his job. Richardson was top goalie as outsiders Brighton won the Autumn Cup but with the arrival of 'Hutch' he was back on the bench.

Archer returned from Winnipeg with a dozen players, amongst them a long lanky gentleman named Les Strongman who, like Beach, was to stay in British hockey for many years, playing for Nottingham and Wembley and later coaching the Panthers. Like the Lovells, the Rosts, the Smiths and the Johnsons, Les too founded a hockey dynasty, his son playing for Nottingham Trojans and his daughter for Peterborough

Ravens. Another in Archer's team who was to become a firm favourite with the fans was ever-smiling Kenny Westman.

The incredible Brighton Tigers were England's Team of the Year even more decisively than Dunfermline had proved to be Scotland's. With the backing of an astute managing-director, C. Roston Bourke, wily player-coach Bobby Lee welded a bunch of 'has-beens' and 'never was-ers' into a fine team. It is worth studying the line-up in detail because at first glance it was a team hell-bent for the cellar rather than the title.

There were no problems in goal. Gib Hutchinson had long since proved himself and there was 'Nobby' Richardson in reserve. It was after this that the troubles started. Lee had two other men, apart from himself, with League experience – Jimmy Chappell and Gordie Poirier. The rest were mainly Canadians who had served in the armed forces in Europe, played hockey at Brighton and liked it. Some had married English girls.

Of this motley crew only one, Frank 'Casey' Stangle, a broken-nosed veteran of the hockey wars, had played top senior hockey in Canada. There was a chubby rearguard with a reasonable hockey background, Bill Booth, who went back home for demob then returned to Brighton; a rough tough blocker named Al Truelove; a quiet, long and lanky centre 'Lefty' Wilmot; and two wingers, Lennie Baker and Lee Thorne. To round out this incongruous crew was another defenceman, Bill Davies, who had played in goal for Wembley during the 1939–40 season.

Lee was a shrewd hockey strategist, had a great sense of humour and could have gained a degree in man-management. He knew which players to cajole, which to threaten, and which to allow to go their own way. Thorne, a small dark and timid fellow, was terrified of him, but Lee coached him into a sound backchecker who contributed valuable points from time to time.

Baker was just as terrified when he first joined the team. So much so that when on a coach journey to an away match at Wembley he wanted to go to the toilet, he did not like to ask for the coach to be stopped. He held himself in – and ended up having treatment in hospital.

Lennie Baker was an all-action player with a blistering although wildly inaccurate shot. He was also very fast, but when he first joined Tigers there was a standing joke around the circuit: 'Where's Baker?' 'In the corner.' Because, with his head down and going hell-for-leather, the corner was invariably where Baker ended up. Under Lee's tutelage, Baker used his powerful shot less often but to greater effect and learned that there was much more to a rink than the four corners.

That first season Lee made the maximum use of both his team's strengths and weaknesses. 'Duke' Campbell started the season with the Tigers but had to return to Harringay, so Lee converted Poirier into an outstanding defenceman. The scoring was made primarily the responsibility of Lee himself and Chappell, with Poirier adding punch from the points on power-plays and with dangerous rushes like Len Burrage. The second line had to check, check and check. It was a policy that worked, although it may not have done without Lee's personal contribution – he topped the League scorers with 111 points, 26 more than his nearest rival Harringay Racers' winger, Gordie Fashaway.

Lee had a wicked sense of humour. Another fine Harringay winger, Bill Glennie, today manager of the Powderhall Stadium in Edinburgh, wore spectacles at one time, later switching to contact lenses. Lee contrived to dislodge Bill's specs during a scuffle on the boards and then, as he apologised to Bill, 'accidentally' kicked the spectacles away, leaving the hapless Glennie to grope for them.

Another little story that passed into hockey history concerned the time a defenceman named Bill Rooker was signed by Tigers. He warmed the bench game after game until one night he exploded to Bobby, 'When are you going to use me?'

'Take it easy, son,' said Lee, 'I'm saving you.'

'What for?' cried Rooker.

'For the supporters' club dance,' smirked Lee.

They were happy days at Brighton with Cheerleader Charlie Connell and an enthusiastic supporters club. Former heavyweight champion Tommy Farr was a regular spectator, as was football star Don Welsh, then managing Brighton & Hove Albion. Alan Weeks, later to become famous as a TV commentator, was the Tigers' publicity manager – and any other job that needed filling, including singing in the summer ice shows.

So much for Brighton – a classic illustration of how a good coach and sound managerial back-up can get the best out of ordinary players.

In 1946–47 the United States, under the guidance of newspaperman, Herb Ralby, were in Britain, playing twenty matches against English and Scottish sides. The Americans were not a terribly strong side – defenceman Gus Galipeau who afterwards played with Racing Club de Paris was probably the best – and won only five of their matches. They had bad luck with injuries and at different times had to borrow Odie Hallowell (who was American-born), Rheal Savard, 'Red' Linton and others from British teams. Little Johnnie Meoli was their only netman and when he was under the weather Ralby was so desperate that he had Drackett stand by – than which there can be no greater desperation! But I still have my team badge and shut-out club medal.

Switzerland were also visiting, led by Hans and Pic Cattini and Bibi Torriani, still good players but no longer quite the force they had been before the war. The *Ice Hockey World* Swiss correspondent, Charlie Gerst, a Davos hairdresser by trade, was on defence. Charlie was a big lad and liked to play Canadian-style. Torriani was still the dominant personality in the team and I had the impression that when he was on the ice the rest deferred to him too much. Anyway, they lost two of their three matches with England, and Brighton trounced them 14–5.

Tigers were the only British team to venture abroad that season, winning four and losing three matches in Czechoslovakia. The Czechs, despite all their troubles, were fanatical about their hockey in those days. When we were there, the little town of Budejovice sent a deputation to Prague asking us to play an extra unscheduled fixture. As the team bus nosed its way down to the rink we passed scores of people carrying ladders, and when we got to the rink we saw why. The rink was

Brighton Tigers, 1946–47, National League Champions. Left to right: 'Nobby' Richardson, Billy Booth, Jimmy Chappell, Lee Thorne, Lennie Baker, Bobby Lee (player-coach), 'Casey' Stangle, Gordie Poirier, Al Truelove, Bill Davies, 'Lefty' Wilmot, Gib Hutchinson.

surrounded by trees and they used the ladders to climb up into the branches for a better view; and this on a winter's night with the temperature below freezing.

Cambridge University undertook a tour of Scotland, but the great days of Varsity hockey were long gone and the undergraduates were well trounced in seven matches, all with Scottish junior teams.

Ice Hockey World All Stars defeated Fife Flyers and Scottish All Stars, but the Scots could take consolation in the fact that the *World* squad also beat Brighton.

The biggest drama was at season's end with play-offs for the London Cup. Both Harringay teams were in the semi-finals, but the management apparently thought so little of their chances that no further matches were scheduled for the Arena. Racers upset the applecart first by qualifying for the final, but nobody worried too much because in the other semi-final Greyhounds were trailing Tigers 7−1 after the first leg and the second leg was at Brighton.

Wyn Cook, the Greyhound captain, was a close friend of mine. When he found that his team were going to be left to their own devices for the second leg, he asked me to travel down in the team coach. On the way we did what only a couple of lunatics could have contemplated, we worked out a strategy to pull back six goals and go on to win. We based it upon well-established Nicklin ideas. The second line of Morgan, Saint and Eizenzoph were no all stars so they were told to keep checking. Any goals scored on them and they would be dead men. The first line of Cook, Glennie and Ricard would do the scoring. Glennie always was a two-way skater but it was gently suggested to Wyn that he would have to do some forechecking if the plan was going to work.

Lussier was a consistent netman and could be relied upon. In front of him Frank Kuly was a good young defenceman of great potential who knew no way of playing other than at one hundred per cent. However, a little chat was necessary with his partner, Montreal-born Guy Bourgeois. Guy was a joker (his impression of Jerry Colonna was hilarious) but his Eastern Canada sense of humour was not always appreciated by his team-mates, most of whom hailed from Western Canada, especially the song he was always singing about 'Portage La Prairie on a Saturday night'. When he concentrated on his hockey he was a talented player, so we asked him to give his all that night.

Most of the team were young and on their first trip to England. Having agreed the game plan there didn't seem much point in working them up to a state of tension, so we went over

The wedding of Alan Weeks to ice show star, Jane Huckle. Best man Bobby Lee can be seen just behind the happy groom.

to the fun-fair opposite the rink and bounced around on the dodgems for an hour.

That night Greyhounds wrote a little hockey history. Tigers were over-confident, and with a 7–1 lead who could have blamed them. Bourgeois and Cook played like heroes – I can still see them hanging over the barrier at the end, sweat streaming from them, panting their lungs out – and Glennie and Ricard really flew. Greyhounds won 11–3 to take the series 12–10 on aggregate.

That really put the cat among the pigeons. Two homeless teams had qualified for the Cup Final! What should have been a show-piece was put on at 6.30 p.m. Thursday 1 May 1947, prior to a Wembley All Stars v. Streatham game. As sunlight streamed through the windows of the Empire Pool, Greyhounds galloped to a 10–3 triumph over Racers. There was no formal cup presentation, just beer and sandwiches in the dressing room. 'Wyn' stuck a large Havana in my mouth – 'for the only coach who ever trained his team on the dodgems'.

I never asked him, and he never asked me, if we really thought Brighton could be beaten that night as we went south on the coach. And it was a long while before I could look Bobby Lee in the eye!

There was hockey in the summer of 1947 at Wembley. Former Monarch defenceman Jack Wilkinson brought over a side

The team that trained for a London Cup upset on the dodgems; Harringay Greyhounds' Lorne Lussier, Bill Glennie and Ricky Ricard at the wheel.

labelled 'Ottawa All Stars', mostly juniors from Inkerman Rockets, plus one or two the professionals had their eyes on and a couple of old Harringay favourites, Joe Shack and Jake Brunning. These two signed again for Harringay in due course, and Wembley recruited a young defenceman named Don Thomson and a likely-looking centre, Jean-Paul Lafortune.

After starting slowly, Ottawa played thirteen matches, three of them against teams chosen by Wembley patrons, winning nine of them.

To almost everyone's surprise, Brighton's creaking veterans successfully retained the National League Championship the following season after Harringay Racers and Streatham had taken the Autumn Cup and National Tournament respectively.

Bobby Lee relied mainly upon the same players, the only newcomers being Frank Trottier's younger brother, Lorne, and ex-Streatham forward, Tommy Durling. Both scored well in the League. It was remarkable that Lorne Trottier could play hockey at all. As a prisoner-of-war he had been forced to march hundreds of miles through Arctic conditions by the Germans and sometimes still felt the effect of those traumatic days.

This was a year, in retrospect, when ice hockey managements began to act like football clubs. 'Sandy' Archer resigned as coach at Nottingham, 'Lou' Bates resigned from Wembley, and Freddie Sutherland was put in charge of Lions. Greyhound fans were not too happy to see Lussier, Campbell, Glennie and Ricard in Racer kit and even more unhappy that their team finished in the cellar.

Greyhounds may not have been much of a hockey club, but

Wyn Cook holds the Cup after Greyhounds had surprisingly beaten Tigers and Racers.

they were certainly colourful characters. Jake Brunning was usually in charge, coach Duke Macdonald often being with his other team, the Racers. The first instructions to the stick boy were always to get in the after-match beer.

Centreman Clair Gratton was one of the few to wear a crash helmet in those days, and it was generally suspected that it was to hide the baldness of his cranium. Clair didn't look a day under fifty and used to sit in the dressing-room smoking a pipe. Greyhounds had an outstanding centreman, boyish Bobby Dennison, and one night before a match he sported a prominent black eye. To an enquiring pressman Jake gave a lengthy explanation of how Bobby had fallen and hit his head on the dressing-room table, even pointing to the exact spot. The effect, however, was rather spoiled by the fact that two of his teammates were still trying to hold down winger Eddie Blondin. Blondin was a fireball, on and off the ice, and a great favourite with the fans. It is said that one night in Ottawa when Eddie picked on a guy far too big for him, the entire Blondin family piled over the boards to his rescue.

One night Blondin crashed head-first into a Wembley goalpost. Coach Duke Macdonald thought he had concussion. 'Are you OK Eddie?' he asked.

'Sure I am' said Eddie.

'What day is it?' asked Macdonald.

'Saturday' replied Eddie.

'What's the score?' said Macdonald.

'We're winning 3–2,' answered Eddie.

'You're OK' breathed a relieved Macdonald.

'Sure I am' chirped Blondin, skating away and lining up with the *Wembley* defence.

Doug 'Bugs Bunny' Young was warming the Greyhound bench at that time. One night Coach Macdonald yelled, 'Doug'. Doug jumped up eager to join the fray.

'Doug,' said Macdonald, 'Jake Brunning's broken his stick — give him yours.'

Macdonald tried blackboard lectures to pep up that team. One day he said, 'We're in over their blue-line, two of our forwards are covered and the defence isn't backing up. Doug, what would you do?'

'Well coach,' said Doug, 'I would slide along the bench a bit in order to be able to see better.'

Doug Young was a great humorist, a tonic in any dressing-room. A versatile player, he was better than the average English born-and-bred at the time but, alas for him, not quite the calibre of Arthur Green, Johnny Oxley and one or two others, including his own pal, Ted Hallam, who later played senior hockey in the States.

As characters go there was never one to equal Johnny Beauchamp, known to one and all as 'The Beauch'. He was another of that group of eccentrics Jake Brunning brought over one year. 'I'm very highly strung,' he would tell people, 'and my father was hanged too.' Which was a gross libel on his parent, a distinguished figure in Canadian political circles.

He was too eccentric for Harringay who asked the BIHA to find him another team. I was taking London All Stars to play Racing Club in Paris and we took 'The Beauch' along for a trial. He played a few games for Racing Club and was a better player than some they had, but Pete Bessone was in charge on the ice and, rough, tough ex-professional that he was, Johnny's sense of humour did not appeal.

Falkirk were looking for a defender, but coach Nelson M'Cuaig's sense of humour made Pete Bessone seem the Bob Hope of the Great Ice Way.

Jack Wake, the Kirkcaldy manager, usually a level-headed sort of fellow, decided to give Beauchamp a trial. Flyers had a brilliant All Star defenceman, Floyd Snider. Light but skilful and one of the best ever to play in Scotland, Floyd didn't take kindly to being told what was wrong with his game by Johnny. So Johnny sat in the stands at Kirkcaldy home games yelling 'We want The Beauch. We want The Beauch.'

One night when Greyhounds were playing Brighton, that great player Gordie Poirier took exception to the way Johnny was throwing his elbows around.

'Beauchamp,' snorted Gordie, 'there are two things which don't go in this rink and unnecessary roughness is one of them.'

'And you are the other,' smirked The Beauch.

He eventually went back to Canada, still swearing he was the greatest hockey player ever, still being laughed at.

They were at the summer shack by the lake, Johnny, his brother's small children and other relatives. A paraffin stove went up in flames. There was no time to get everyone out and the timber shack was a fire-trap. Johnny 'The Beauch' picked up that flaming stove and ran outside with it. He saved his family's lives at the cost of his own. Wherever Johnny Beauchamp is now, no one is laughing at him any more.

Courage of another kind was shown in 1948 by referee Sammy Rosen. Rosen, an extrovert character who had played briefly in goal at Wembley before becoming an arbiter, was never afraid to do something out of the ordinary and on this particular occasion he reversed a decision after fresh evidence from the timekeepers.

Poirier was out for six weeks that season with a fractured jaw. Panthers and Greyhounds played a match short in the National Tournament after the former, in Paris for an exhibition match, had been caught up in a French railway strike and could not get back in time. As the match did not affect the final standings, the BIHA waived it.

In the League, Ernie Leacock, by far the best referee of them all, gave Streatham's very good goalie Monty Reynolds (something of a shut-out king when he was with Chatham Maroons) two minutes for clipping Racer Bill Glennie. George Baillie went in goal but was beaten twice. Fortunately, there were no hotheads around to bring about a repetition of the 1939 affair. Leacock, who came over originally as a player in the early 1930s, saved at least one life during his subsequent refereeing career. Wembley Lions' defenceman Joe Watts went down hard without any other player being near him. He had had a fit, but only Leacock was quick-witted enough to realise that the player was swallowing his tongue. He put a finger in Watts' mouth and hooked the tongue back. The medics said Joe undoubtedly owed his life to that speedy action.

Tigers apart, Racers and Streatham were the season's best clubs. Stapleford had a power-house in South London with three forwards in the League's top ten — pre-war favourite captain 'Chuck' Turner, a big wingman Bud McEachren, and a crafty centre Dave Miller. Tall Paddy Ryan was an excellent defender.

Another player recruited that season must be mentioned in

any history of the game. During the off-season, 'Sandy' Archer, back in Winnipeg to replace the weak links in his Nottingham side, had recruited some useful-looking men including a centre of excellent repute. However, forty-eight hours before the party was due to leave for England, the centreman pulled out. Archer, at his wit's end, grabbed the first player he could find, a skinny, undersized and undernourished Ukrainian youngster called Victor Zamick. 'I thought I was crazy to take a chance on him. I was sure he would be a failure,' Archer was to say later.

Nottingham officials who met the boat thought Archer was crazy too. At first they did not realise that this ill-at-ease youngster was one of their new players. When they were told they nearly collapsed of shock.

By 1955 Victor, better-known now as 'Chick', was the outstanding player in Europe, the only man in the world to have scored over 600 goals in a senior league. With left-winger Les Strongman and coach Archie Stinchcombe (who succeeded Archer) he brought two National League Championships to the Midlands, and when Stinchcombe retired in the summer of 1955, he took over as player-coach. And it all happened because another player changed his mind and stayed home in Canada.

Dundee Tigers, after a poor start to the season, defeated the champions, Dunfermline, in a play-off for the League Championship and added the Canada Cup to their laurels for good measure. Two men made the difference as far as Tigers were concerned. Weakness in the nets was repaired by the signing of former Wembley Monarch goalie George Kovac and on defence by persuading the temperamental Norman Gustavsen, who had been reluctant to sign again, to put pen to paper.

Only Gustavsen's mercurial nature prevented him being as good a rearguard as Art Hodgins. They were two very tough men, and other players would recount in awe how one off-season the two allegedly sat opposite each other at a table and took it in turns to hit one another, the first to quit losing the bet. They both ended out for the count.

Tigers were coached by old-timer Laurie Marchant. Two other players who had vital roles were skipper Robbie Burns and top scorer Johnny Evans.

Falkirk, winners of the League consolation trophy, the Bairns, and runners-up in the Scottish Autumn and the Canada Cups, were the other team of note, with a good goalie, Hap Finch, and a forward who knew his way to goal, Johnny Savicky, as their outstanding players.

Internationally, 1947–48 was an interesting season and Scotland had better reason than most for being pleased with life.

The Great Britain team for the 1948 Olympics was truly representative and included Tuck Syme (Dunfermline), Bert Smith (Fife) and Frankie Jardine (Glasgow Mohawks). Three of the 1936 Triple Crown team – Chappell, Davey and Stinchcombe – remained, and Stinchcombe was made captain. English and Scottish League veterans Frankie Green, Freddie Dunkelman and George Baillie, Brighton newcomer Lennie Baker and English born-and-bred players, 'Stan' Simon, Johnny Oxley, Arthur Green and Johnny Murray completed the squad.

The team warmed up by competing in the Devred Cup in Switzerland against the Polish national team, Arosa and Neuchatel, winning all three games to take the trophy. Neuchatel were beaten 6–5 in the final game, Stinchcombe scoring the winning goal in overtime.

The Olympics were a tougher proposition. Nearly abandoned when two American teams turned up, one from the Amateur Athletic Union, the other from the Amateur Hockey Association, the Olympic title was regained by Canada, with Czechoslovakia as runners-up. The problem of the two American teams was solved by the AAU team marching in the parade and the AHA team actually playing. After this, control of the sport went from the AAU into the hands of the AHA.

Canada were represented by RCAF Flyers and were not expected to win. Coached by Frankie Boucher, of the great Boucher hockey dynasty, who had played in England during the war and subsequently coached at Wembley, they squeezed home on goal average.

Britain fought hard against Canada before losing 3–0. The Czechs were in fine form and Britain took an 11–4 beating, despite goals from Frankie Green, Baillie, Stinchcombe and Arthur Green. Frankie Green, Davey and Baker scored against Sweden, but the Scandinavians eked out a close 4–3 win.

The British team took out their frustrations on Italy with a 14–7 bonanza, Frankie Green (4), Oxley (4), Baker (2), Chappell, Murray, Davey and Jardine getting the goals. Austria were beaten 5–4 (Baker 2, Arthur Green, Chappell and Oxley) and Poland 7–2, not surprisingly after Britain's 10–4 win in the Devred Cup over the same team.

Defeat by Switzerland (12–3) who were coached by former Harringay Greyhound captain and centre-ice 'Wyn' Cook, relegated Great Britain to sixth of nine clubs. However, for an all-British-born, largely home-bred team it was an encouraging campaign.

Better was to come from a Scottish viewpoint. Towards the end of the season Canada (RCAF Flyers), Czechoslovakia, France (Racing Club de Paris) and Scotland (League All Stars) met in Paris to contest the Jean Potin Cup. The Czechs, despite being European Champions, failed to win a match, the other teams each won two and lost one, and France, who scored the most goals, were ajudged the winners.

Scotland beat Canada, the Olympic Champions, 2−1, Johnny Savicky and Randy Ellis scoring the goals. A very good Scottish team comprised: Belanger (Glasgow Bruins) in goal; Hodgins (Paisley Pirates), Snider (Fife Flyers), Herb Kewley (Dunfermline Vikings) and Gustavsen (Dundee Tigers) on defence; Randy Ellis (Dunfermline Vikings), Thaler (Paisley Pirates), Savicky (Falkirk Lions), Sergnese (Perth Panthers), Gordon (Ayr Raiders) and Evans (Dundee Tigers) as forwards.

Czechoslovakia, Canada and USA all visited Britain during the season, as did club sides from Czechoslovakia, Sweden and France, Harringay Greyhounds went to Czechoslovakia and Tigers to Switzerland. There were twenty-four matches between English and Scottish senior clubs, the English winning nineteen and drawing one.

Earls Court Rangers returned to the English National League in 1948−49, but the headlines were snatched by Racers who, captained by the veteran 'Duke' Campbell, now playing on defence, finished eleven points ahead of Streatham. Racers' first

Ottawa All Stars came over in the summer of 1947 bringing new and old faces. 'Lou' Bates (in suit) and 'Sonny' Rost present tankards to Ottawa coach, Jack Wilkinson, long-time friend of Bates and himself a former Wembley defender. Harvey Bennett, Ottawa goalie, awaits his turn.

'The skinny undersized Ukrainian kid' who became one of the greatest of all time; 'Chick' Zamick (left) reunited with post-war hockey's other great scorer, George Beach.

'Red' Stapleford coaching some of his Streatham players in 1948. Left to right: Ross Richardson, Verne Gardiner, Monty Reynolds, George Drysdale, Dave Miller, Larry McKay, Norm Gardiner and 'Red'.

line of Joe Shack, Bill Glennie and Pete Payette finished first, second and third in the League scoring with 69, 66, and 57 points respectively in a 28-game schedule, beating the prolific 'Chick' Zamick, of Nottingham, into fourth place.

Archie Stinchcombe was now coaching Panthers, with the Nottingham Club's former coach, Archer, back at Wembley. His Monarchs took both the Autumn Cup and the International Tournament, the latter being truly international once more with the inclusion of Paris, although the Frenchmen won only one match. Racers, on tour for some of the time, did not take part.

Monarchs were a good side with Mason in goal, Rost, 'Red' Kurz, Don Thomson and Roy Thompson on defence, experienced forwards in Frank Trottier and Freddie Sutherland with George Beach at centre, and another 'Kid Line' of Mauno Kauppi, Jean-Paul Lafortune and Les Anning. 'Mac' McLachlan was also a regular.

Streatham were the pick of the rest. Reynolds was back in the nets and he had four big men guarding the blue-line: 'Doc' Brodrick, Paddy Ryan, Art Hodgins (who had finally succumbed to the lures of English teams) and English-born and Wembley-trained Doug Wilson.

Wilson was a big, rough fellow who could hold his own in a tussle with anyone, but he spoke with awe of the aggressive spirit of some of the Scots-born players, notably chunky Joe Brown, of Paisley. 'I was in the corner after the puck when I heard what I took to be the snorting of a rhino right behind me. It was Joe Brown. I thought if you want the puck that bad, mate, you have it. And I got the hell out of there.'

Wilson was an interesting character. He was a product of the pre-war Wembley junior training scheme in which his father, known to all and sundry as 'Pop', was a leading figure. His countenance was craggy to say the least, and it had not been improved by various collisions, encounters with sticks and barriers and so on. At the last count he had had 103 stitches inserted in his face, truly a map of hockey history. One night at Wembley he dived at an opponent, missed and crashed face-first into the boards – that cost him sixteen stitches. A fortnight later he crashed into a goal-post at Durham and needed seven more. None of his misfortunes ever dampened his spirits, however; he was the sort of humorist every team needs.

For part of the season Streatham also had Gustavsen, but big 'Moose' decided to go back to Canada and eventually signed professional forms with St Paul Saints.

Fife Flyers finished top of the regular schedule in the Scottish League, but Falkirk Lions won the play-offs and Perth took the Consolation Tournament. Lions also won the Scottish and Canada Cups and were undoubtedly Scotland's Team of the Year. Pat Casey, joined by brother Phil, were Lions' top scorers over the regular schedule, but as captain Gordon McPhail, Rennie Platt and Lionel Tremblay were also in the top twelve, Lions, coached by English and Scottish League veteran, George McNeil, were obviously a well-balanced team.

Flyers owed much to the sometimes sensational scoring of

Falkirk Lions, Scotland's best play-off team of the 1940s and 1950s. This dressing room group includes Pat Casey, Gord Blackman, Johnny Savicky and Hap Finch.

Popping in the goals for Britain's 1948 Olympic team was centre, Frankie Green, of Wembley and Southampton.

Bud Scrutton and Chic Mann, although when Paisley netman Ian Orr saved two penalty shots on 17 February 1949, the red-faced 'sharpshooters' were Scrutton and Mann. Orr made a little bit of history in more ways than one. Pirates started the season with a Canadian netminder, John Placentine, but Scots born-and-bred Orr displaced him and played most of the season.

Bert Smith and Jimmy Mitchell at Kirkcaldy and defender Bill Sneddon at Falkirk were other native Scots who did well.

It was a year when British players were given great encouragement at all Scottish rinks, and at Durham, Harringay (where Duke Macdonald ran 5 a.m. practices), Streatham (where 'Doc' Brodtick was in charge) and at Brighton (with Billy Booth, later to coach at Durham, handling matters). *Ice Hockey World* reporter Greg Ward persuaded the Richmond management to let him run coaching classes on Tuesday nights, and Wembley and Streatham both staged under-12 matches as curtain-raisers to League games.

The BIHA gave an Intermediate Cup, the semi-finalists being the RAF, Wembley, Streatham and Sussex. Wembley, led by international Johnny Murray, defeated the RAF 3–2 in the final, and the Cup was presented by Marshal of the RAF, Lord Tedder.

The Canadian Navy (represented by the 'Magnificent') also played matches at Empress Hall, Streatham and Wembley against the RAF and Wembley Intermediates.

Four thousand people packed Durham every week to see Wasps play the pick of Scottish and English intermediate teams, including a Northern Tournament involving the Scottish clubs.

The Durham Rink was packed every Saturday to see the local Wasps, then an intermediate side. Standing, left to right: Bill Britt Snr (secretary), Joe Stephenson, Russ Proudfoot, Gord Belmore, Jimmy Hall, Fred Vine, Ronny Sancaster, Bob Thompson, Bob Cartwright, John Smith (manager), Bobby Bruin. Kneeling: Bill Britt Jnr, Gerry Gibson, 'Flash' Lynn, Earl Carlson and Mike Davey (coach).

Dunfermline knocked Durham out of the play-offs when Johnny Rolland scored after fifteen minutes and forty seconds of overtime.

Off the ice, Sam McNabney, of Perth Panthers, was awarded £2,050 for the partial loss of an eye following a playing accident. McNabney became coach at Ayr.

Czechoslovakia won the World and European Championships. Canada (represented by Sudbury Wolves) lost the vital game 3–2. From a British fan's viewpoint, it was interesting that Canada had three former Scottish League men – Bob Mills, Herb Kewley and John Kovich.

A great name disappeared from the scene in 1949–50 with Harringay's decision to run only one team – so Greyhounds faded into limbo.

Not all the news was bad. The Murrayfield, Edinburgh, rink, built in 1939 and promptly requisitioned, was to be freed by the Government. Southampton had permission to rebuild on the site of their bombed rink, and Grimsby, re-formed the previous season, intended to continue the development of hockey locally. Durham intended continuing, Liverpool hoped to continue, Manchester and Blackpool might come back into the picture. All was not lost!

It was fitting that Streatham, senior survivors of the National League, should turn out to be England's Team of the Year. Racers set a hot pace to win the Autumn Cup, Streatham won the National Tournament while Harringay were touring the Continent and then came from behind to win the League title

'Red' Stapleford liked intelligent players of good character like André Charest, a dentist on post-graduate studies, here in action against Harringay's top netman, 'Pete' Belanger, formerly with Glasgow and Fife.

for the first time in fifteen years. Salaries in general were higher than ever, a number of players getting £25 a week or more. One was paid £22.10s. for playing and also paid to manage the rink skate shop. Yet it was Streatham, one of the lowest-paid teams in the circuit, who won the Championship.

Harvey 'Red' Stapleford, Streatham's coach, was a remarkable man. As a player he lived up to his red hair and was something of a fiery competitor. As a coach he was brilliant, although still working on a short fuse. Most of his players learned to keep a low profile when 'Red' was on the rampage. At the tail-end of his playing career when he had already taken up the coaching reins, I was sitting in the Streatham dressing-room after the South Londoners had just suffered a defeat at the hands of Racers. 'Red' was in the shower when the Harringay timekeeper, a keen type named Matthews, walked in. There had been some arguments with him during the game and he would have done well to keep his head down for a while, but he wanted the match-sheet signed and in he came, beaming all over his face. 'Red' came out of the shower, naked as the day he was born, saw Matthews and went mad. Matthews beat a hasty retreat and 'Red', still without a stitch on, chased him down the corridor.

Away from ice hockey, Stapleford was an articulate, educated and highly intelligent man who eventually became Industrial and Trades Commissioner for Ontario with an office in the West End of London. He married a daughter of one of the famous Palladium 'Crazy Gang', and their daughter, Sally, became British Champion ice-skater.

Stapleford's main strength as a coach lay in his ability to attract the right type of player. He liked big, strong skaters but he also liked them to have some intelligence. 'Doc' Brodrick, for example, was not only a good rearguard but he was also a qualified doctor on post-graduate research. Andre Charest and Gordie Knutson, two sharp forwards, were dentists, also engaged in post-graduate studies. Bill Winemaster, who later played for Racers, was an engineering student who eventually became chief of Perkins Diesel operations in Canada.

There were few newcomers on Stapleford's Championship squad. Brodrick was captain, Ryan and Hodgins were back with him on defence and George Drysdale, Dave Miller, George Baillie, Jimmy Campbell and Johnny Sergnese were again on duty up-front. However, four of the six newcomers were winners. Keith Woodall in the nets made the fans forget Monty Reynolds. In attack Mike Yaschuk was Streatham's leading scorer in the League, and big Kenny Campbell, late of Montreal

Royals and Earls Court Rangers, brought top-class finesse to the team. Burly George Edwards was another hit.

Stapleford always put the emphasis on playing for the team rather than on individual glory, and Streatham won the League despite not having a player in the first seventeen in the scoring list. Apart from Rangers, who scored only 86 goals, Streatham were the lowest scoring club with 96, yet they only conceded 86. Rangers, who finished bottom, had the second-best defence, conceding 100 goals.

Zamick led the League scorers, and Panthers had two more men in the top ten, one of them being defenceman Kenny Westman, which may help to explain why the defence leaked like a sieve. No less than 151 goals were pumped past the hapless Dick Halverson and back-up goalie, Alan Watson, and Panthers finished one from the bottom.

The Scottish National League was almost a repeat performance of the previous season, with McNeil's Falkirk Lions taking the Championship after Flyers had once more headed the regular schedule. Perth again took the consolation award.

Lions had the backbone of their previous winning team: tubby Hap Finch in the nets, the Casey brothers, Archie Katzman, and some very good Scots boys in Sneddon, Carlyle, Paton and Nicholson. As a bonus, Canadian newcomer Milt Carrigan was named Rookie of the Year.

There were money troubles in Scotland, but this time no threat of strike action. The devaluation of the pound lowered

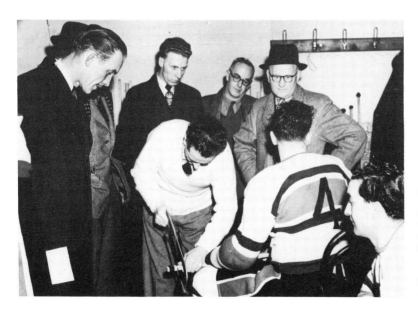

In the 1950 World Championships in London, referee Hauser (Switzerland) said 'Tiny' Syme's stick was two inches too long. Trainer Jock Muldoon saws off the offending inches watched by coach 'Lou' Bates, the author (partially hidden by Bates), Scotland's ace coach George McNeil, 'Jock' Robin, ill-fated goalie of Earls Court Marlboroughs, and 'Doc' McCabe, of the SIHA. The other British player is Ray Hammond, of Sussex.

the value of the players' salaries almost as soon as they arrived in Scotland, but an amicable settlement was reached.

Internationally, the highlight was the staging of the World and European Championships in London (Wembley, Harringay and Earls Court) after an absence of thirteen years. Great Britain, coached by the immortal 'Lou' Bates, went into the Championships with high hopes, despite the fact that every man on the team was British born-and-bred. Led by Falkirk's Ken Nicholson, the home team headed their first round pool by defeating France 9−0 and Norway 2−0. They followed up in the final by again beating Norway, this time 4−3 and also beating Sweden 5−4.

The crucial game was that against USA, who Great Britain had already beaten 4−0 in an exhibition match. It was a stormy affair, there were some strange refereeing decisions and, it has to be said, some of the Scottish boys lost their heads. The result was the Americans won 3−2.

Canada, represented by the Edmonton Waterloo Mercurys, were breezing past all opposition and they proceeded to crush Britain 12−0. Britain still had a chance of the European title when USA obligingly defeated Switzerland, but the team had lost their initial spark and tamely submitted 10−3 to finish fourth of nine nations.

British players were generally encouraged throughout the season with local leagues at many rinks. The first-ever junior international took place at Richmond on Whit Monday, 29 May 1950, Scotland beating England 4−1 in a thrilling match. All the players were under eighteen, but the greater experience of the Scots − five of them had played for League clubs − told in the end.

Wembley won the English Junior League. Coached by Johnny Murray, their captain was Gordon English, a netman who later played senior League hockey.

The RAF, coached by Wembley Monarchs' defenceman Roy Thompson, again won the English Intermediate League. They had a real enthusiast in their captain, Dave Evans, a serving officer.

Ayr Spitfires were the best juniors in Scotland, winning the Mitchell, Frame and Banner trophies with Falkirk taking the Young Cup and the Silver Pucks, and a clean-play trophy going to Kirkcaldy. While Scottish pee-wees had a competition of their own, which was won by Perth Panther Cubs.

Streatham Royals defeated Earls Court Marlboroughs in the final play-offs of the Liverpool Amateur Tournament, and at Grimsby there were four junior teams in addition to the intermediate Red Wings. Red Wings captain, Reg Mason, had been with the team since hockey began at the rink in 1935.

The BIHA staged a Junior Knock-out Tournament at Richmond, Wembley Colts defeating Streatham Indians 2−0 in the final.

Durham Wasps, coached by ex-Brighton Billy Booth, not only headed the Northern Tournament schedule but beat Paisley Wildcats in the final play-off for the BIHA Cup. How many present-day Wasp fans would recognise this line-up? Jimmy Carlisle; Billy Booth, Bobby Thompson, George Thompson, Ray Hayes, Alan Waddell, Ian Dobson, Mike Jackson, Gordie Belmore, Joe Bell, Bobby Cartwright, Ronnie Sancaster, Earl Carlson. Belmore was Wasps' principal stinger, ably backed by the idols of the local crowd, Earl Carlson and Ray 'Ace' Hayes, with Booth and Sancaster providing a resolute defence.

All in all, 1949−50 was the best season yet for native hockey talent.

On the senior front, the BIHA took a firm line with miscreants. Bob Kaye and Gordie Miller were suspended for the season (effective in Canada) when they accepted offers from Harringay, flew over and decided to go back after one game. The story was an *Ice Hockey World* scoop, following a chance meeting with the pair. Readers knew the two were homeward-bound before many people at Harringay.

'Red' Kurz, Wembley Monarch defenceman who had twice made the All Star B team, was suspended for the following season after an incident in a Wembley v. The Rest exhibition once the regular season had ended. Kurz had had a fine season and it was a great pity. A quiet gentle man off the ice, 'Red' made a come-back to star in the Scottish League.

Gib Hutchinson, the sometimes irascible Brighton netman, was suspended for the rest of the current season, and a number of other players received short suspensions or fines.

The funniest disciplinary incident concerned Dunfermline's fiery little forward, 'Nebby' Thrasher. Thrasher was too small to offer his opponents violence so he tried talking them to death. Against Perth, his constant yapping earned him 42 minutes in penalties.

Streatham set up a remarkable unbeaten sequence in playing 24 home games without defeat. Starting 21 December when they beat Rangers 5−2, they remained unbeaten until 26 April when they lost 6−4 to Tigers.

And, at last, the Scottish League defeated the English League.

Hockey attendances remained good in 1950–51 despite money shortages and the Korean war. It was also the year when Nottingham Panthers came good. They all laughed at coach Archie Stinchcombe when he declaimed, 'This is the best team I ever had'. They laughed even more five weeks later when Panthers held up all the other clubs in the Autumn Cup. The laughs were a little uneasy when Panthers recovered enough to challenge Tigers for the trophy, and Archie did all the laughing when his team pipped the selfsame Tigers to win the Championship for the first time.

The pride of Nottingham were: Ken Johnson (from Ayr); Bill Allen, Pete Moulden, Bill McDonald, Gerry Watson, 'Chick' Zamick, Bill Ringer, Les Strongman (captain), Pat Casey (from Falkirk), Johnny Pyryhora, Gyle Woods and 'Bud' James.

'Chick' Zamick was once again the scoring champion, All Star A centre and the League's 'Most Popular Player'. Perhaps more significant was the fact that in a sporting city like Nottingham he was voted 'Sportsman of the Year' in face of competition from England cricketers like Reg Simpson and Joe Hardstaff, goal-scoring forwards Wally Ardron and Tommy Lawton and Channel swimmer Tom Blower.

British hockey suffered a sad loss when Earls Court Rangers centreman Walter Risi was killed in a car crash shortly after signing for Rangers again. Kenny Booth wore Risi's shorts for the first game of the season and said, 'I'm going to get a goal for Wally,' and he did.

'Duke' Campbell moved across London from Harringay to Earls Court to become player-coach of Rangers; Les Anning made a come-back with the same team. Don Callaghan went from Wembley to Streatham; Kenny Campbell and Bud McEachren from Streatham to Harringay; Tiger 'Lefty' Wilmot lined up with Lions; Lion Freddie Sutherland moved to Brighton; British boy 'Fish' Robertson got a chance in the Harringay nets and did well. He was another goalie to come from the Sussex team which had already produced Reg Merriefield and 'Nobby' Richardson.

A boy who sued Harringay after being struck in the eye by a puck lost his case. In Washington, a woman who sued the local ice rink in similar circumstances was awarded £6,000.

Television covered matches at Harringay, Wembley and Empress Hall; fog caused postponement of a game between Cambridge University and the Civil Service; Gordie Poirier came out of retirement to play for Racers; and a grateful Czech Government threw eight members of the national team into jail after two others had defected — it was all happening.

Things were also happening in Scotland. Paisley headed the regular League schedule and then broke with precedent by winning the play-offs too. On the surface it was down to the scoring performances of baby-faced Stu Robertson and his mates, Bob Kelly and Ken Head, but it owed a lot to some quick, decisive surgery by manager Peter M'Kenzie.

Faced with a struggling team and a half-empty rink, he fired Tommy Lauder as coach (the veteran moving on to star on the Perth defence) and to everyone's surprise replaced him with former rearguard and referee, 'Red' Thomson, a stern disciplinarian. Then he signed Bernie Hill from Harringay Racers to bolster the blue-line. The signing served two purposes: it strengthened Paisley's defence; and it brought back fans who remembered Hill from when he played at Paisley a couple of seasons previously. Skipper Elwood Shell, rated a joker, turned in the best hockey of his career under the new regime and was voted All Star; Kelly was made 'Rookie of the Year.'

Perth had a good club, coached by Tommy Forgie, ex-Richmond and Brighton forward who later played professional hockey in the United States League; and so did Canada Cup winners Dunfermline. Tuck Syme, who played on defence with brother Tiny, became the first native born-and-bred player to make All Star.

Great Britain's chances were completely ruined in the World Championships by some new eligibility rules whereby Arthur Green, Johnny Oxley, Freddie Dunkelman and 'Fish' Robertson, all English National League players, were barred. With Tuck and Tiny Syme also missing, they could only beat Finland and draw with USA. Canada, represented by Lethbridge Maple Leafs, boosted by a line from Kitchener-Waterloo Flying Dutchmen, swamped all opposition to take the world title.

Canada were led by Dick Gray who, had it not been for the war, would have lined-up with Wembley in the 1939–40 season. Gray was a thinking man very much in the character of the man he looked so much like, film star Randolph Scott. Canada's high scorer was Stan Obodiac, later with Wembley and Ayr, who was publicity manager at the Maple Leaf Gardens, Toronto, at his untimely death. Stan was the author of several books, a wartime pilot with a good record and a man with friends from the highest to the lowest. Terminally ill, he was honoured by the Leafs and asked to face-off the puck to start what was to be his last season.

Canada's other triumph was to be first winners of the Churchill Cup, named after the great statesman with his approval. They came from behind to beat England (League All

Lethbridge Maple Leafs who won the World Championship for Canada in 1951 toured Britain. In an interval of a match against Ayr Raiders, Tom Wood, Billy Gibson and Bill Chandler read *Ice Hockey World*.

Stars) 4–3. Both teams trounced USA, composed largely of French-Americans from New England.

Wembley Terriers were English Intermediate and Northern Amateur Champions. They had a good club – most of them had played or would in future play with League teams – and near season's end they were reinforced by one of British hockey's 'greats' Gordie Poirier, who had his release from Racers.

Incidentally, for those interested in 'how are the mighty fallen', Harringay Racers must have had their worst team of all time. They used at least twenty-three players, including four goalies – Eddie McLeod, 'Red' Jones, 'Fish' Robertson and Doug Young (as practice goalie). Some of their players had never been heard of before – and have not been heard of since. Certainly, it was not a team with the Nicklin stamp on it.

In North West London the following season the glory days returned to Wembley as Lions, master-minded by Frankie Boucher, won the National League title after a gap of fifteen years. Boucher, pale-faced and blond, did not look the part of a tough successful hockey coach despite his World Championship victory with RCAF Flyers, but under that unassuming exterior a lot of the hockey 'know how' of his famous relatives (his uncle was New York Rangers' general manager at the time) had rubbed off. Not that he was any slouch himself, he had played as a professional with Providence, but like so many sportsmen of his generation the war had interrupted his career.

Boucher had a good goalie in Bob Cornforth, but was a little worried about the defence of veteran Clarence 'Sonny' Rost and British-bred Arthur Green and Roy Shepherd, although these two were probably the best English-born defencemen of all time. So he brought over Henri Labrosse, a big French-Canadian, and named himself as cover for the rearguard. 'Sonny' shed his helmet and his moustache and the years with them, and had one of his best seasons.

Scintillating George Beach was at centre on one line, with Harringay centre Bobby Dennison successfully converted to a right-winger on one flank and lanky Mal Davidson on the other. Maguire, Tyrrell and Riopelle made up the second line and 'Lefty' Wilmot was spare forward, Tony Malo being transferred to Nottingham when 'Chick' Zamick was injured.

Davidson did most of the defensive work for high-scoring Beach and Dennison, and he and the equally giraffe-like Wilmot were used to kill-off penalties, the best pair in the League at this task. Both were quiet unassuming men off the ice, but on it they stuck to their men like leeches.

Boucher was rightly voted 'Coach of the Year', and the runner-up was 'Duke' Campbell who cajoled Rangers to their best-ever position in the League in second place, three points behind Lions.

With forwards of the calibre of Kenny Booth, Les Anning, Stan DeQuoy, Fred Denny and Gyle Woods, versatile ex-Harringay star 'Wyn' Cook and former Brighton defender Tommy Jamieson alongside steady Alf Harvey, plus the goal-tending of Ken Dargavel, Rangers were a well-balanced squad.

Streatham took the Autumn Cup and were third in the League, the big man (literally) in their line-up being Earl Betker, a worthy successor to Reynolds and Woodall between the posts. Although with players like Hodgins, the Callaghan brothers, Jack Leckie, Vic Fildes and Ray Maisoneuve, Streatham were hardly a one-man team.

Brighton's Lea Hardy, a fast-skating forward or defender, was England's 'Rookie of the Year'. This likeable fellow married a leading skater, Barbara Wyatt, and their son, born in Switzerland, is playing professional hockey today.

In Scotland, Falkirk Lions again proved themselves a great play-off team after Ayr Raiders had topped the regular schedule. These two teams dominated the season, Ayr winning the Coronation and Autumn Cups, and Falkirk the Canada Cup. Lions defeated Perth in the finals, Fife Flyers winning the consolation tournament.

John Barrie, UK Billiards Champion, demonstrates some shots 'handicapped' by hockey gloves and stick. Watching, left to right, are the author and Streatham players 'Paddy' Ryan, Keith Woodall, Johnny Sergnese and Dave Miller with trainer Sandy Fear (partially hidden by Barrie).

Stu Cruikshank, a top star with Falkirk Lions and later a successful coach in Switzerland, seen (left) with 1951–52 Falkirk team-mates Tom Henry, John Brown and Jim Fiddler.

McNeil was still at the Falkirk helm and earned his money with some shrewd moves to strengthen his squad as the season wore on. Netman Murray Dodd was flown in from Canada and Bob Tripp traded to Paisley, and as the play-offs neared George released Jim Fiddler and former Dundee star George Sinfield, signing Gerry Rose (ex-Dundee and Wembley), Johny Pyryhora (ex-Nottingham) and Syd Arnold (ex-Paisley).

Stu Cruikshank was a key member of that Falkirk team and now runs an International Ice Hockey School in Switzerland. He recalls, somewhat wistfully: 'I guess to compare the Scottish

League of my time with hockey today one has to study the modern game closely. Through TV we receive a lot of the NHL games from America. We see games that don't even resemble good Senior 'A' hockey. One of the reasons appears to be that the referees let the players do anything and we see pulling of arms, legs and sweaters enough to make you think the guys are playing a game which is fifty per cent rugby football.

'In the old days we used to see more neat bodychecks, which was a bit of an art in itself because the referees did not let the players get away with everything. Another of the reasons we have so much pulling, and so on, today is that the difference in skating ability is so great that the slower guy has to compensate for his slowness by pulling at the faster player.

'All this is more noticeable when our Canadian national team is playing against the Russians. On the big ice surfaces, the Russians just waltz into open spots and keep their distance. When a Canadian player rushes at the Russian, the latter just relays a pass to a team-mate and they make us look like real slow pokes.

'Getting back to the NHL and Canadians against Canadians like it was in Scotland and England when we had ten Canadians and a couple of Scottish or English players, I come to the conclusion that a great many guys who played in Great Britain were born thirty to forty years too soon. There were a lot of good hockey players who came over to Europe after the last war because they were not quite good enough to make the NHL (there were only six NHL clubs in those days) and maybe not the American League either, but I am pretty sure that today some of those players would be pretty big stars in the NHL.

'I think of 'Chick' Zamick, Les Strongman, 'Red' Kurz, Bobby Burns, Jim Yeaman, Syd Arnold, Les Anning, Fred Denny, Vic Krekelwetz, Art Hodgins, Ray Maisoneuve, Bill Glennie, Hal Schooley, Ken Doig, Bruce Hamilton, Henry Hayes, Paul Provost, Orville Martini, André Girard, Ernie Domenico, Bobby Lee, Joe Shack, Art Sullivan, Lennie Baker, Bob Kelly, Stu Robertson, 'Moe' Fife, Bobby Dennison, Tommy Forgie, Frankie Boucher, George Beach, 'Sonny' Rost, 'Pete' Belanger, Dave Maguire, 'Rip' Riopelle, Henri Labrosse, Gar Vasey, Whit Mousseau, Herb Kewley, Ray Dinardo, and so many others who played before I came over in 1951.

'A lot of the names of old buddies have slipped my memory over the years, but what I can say is that with all the talented ice hockey players who did not know where to play in Canada during what they call the good old days, the English and Scottish public were treated to some great entertainment by some very good hockey players. The hockey was a lot cleaner and the players used to skate harder knowing that they were not going to get pulled down from the side or from behind – and if they were then the other team would suffer a two-minute penalty which could cost dear.

'In the years just after the war there were a lot of hockey players about who could not make the professional teams so came abroad to play. Today, the professionals come over here to play to get away from all the roughness and stress that is today's hockey. They spend a few years playing professional and then many of them want out as there is too much hassle and travelling, and so on.

'My thoughts about the game in England and Scotland during my period from 1951 to 1956 is that the paying customers were treated to some very good games, the like of which they will have to wait a very long time to see again.

'During those years when players were getting £15 per week compared with £1,500 today, we picked a select team of Canadians playing in Europe, and after the World Championships we beat Canada, Russia and Czechoslovakia at a tournament in Geneva. I've still got the Omega watch each of us was presented with for winning the tournament. The Russians came second. Denny, Martini, Girard, Dennison, Kelly, Fife, Vasey, Dobbin and Wittal were on our team.

'I don't say all this because I was present in those good years, but it does seem to me that the guys gave more than the players of today. Maybe it had something to do with their upbringing as they passed through the war years and things were a bit tougher.'

A number of the players Stu mentions – Herb Kewley, Domenico, Martini, Vasey and Girard – were in the Ayr squad, together with a smart netman, Albert 'Doc' Holliday.

Wembley Terriers ousted Streatham Royals in the English Intermediate League, but Earls Court Marlboroughs defeated Durham Wasps, the regular schedule leaders, in the Northern Amateur play-offs, a good performance on a circuit which included Perth, Kirkcaldy, Falkirk and Glasgow as well as Streatham and Wembley. In retrospect, this competition was a harbinger of the future of British ice hockey.

1951–52 was also a great season for Liverpool Leopards. Headed by Carl Sturtridge, they not only won the Midland League, and the Liverpool and Blackpool Tournaments, but also nine of eleven matches on a Swiss tour.

On a more exalted international level, Canada, represented by Edmonton Mercurys, won the Olympic and World titles.

Great Britain did not take part, but Ernie Leacock was honoured by being the first professional referee asked to officiate at the Olympics. Mind you, he did not get paid – just £15 for expenses.

There was some consolation for missing the Olympics when England, captained by home-grown Arthur Green, defeated Canada and the USA for the Churchill Cup, the BIHA having turned down challenges from Streatham and Ayr. The team that beat USA 11–2 and Canada 6–4 was: 'Pete' Belanger (Harringay Racers) and Bob Cornforth (Wembley Lions) in goal; Bill Johnson and Milt Swindlehurst (Racers), Arthur Green (Lions) (captain) and Tommy Jamieson (Earls Court Rangers) on defence; Kenny Booth, Stan DeQuoy and Les Anning (Rangers); Tony Licari, Bill Glennie and Joe Shack (Racers); Dave Maguire, Ross Tyrrell and Rip Riopelle (Lions); Frankie Boucher (Lions) was coach. Sir Victor Tait, a former England defenceman himself, presented the Cup to Joe Shack, Green having been injured against the Americans.

Even more encouraging for the future of the sport was England's victory in the first-ever European Intermediate Championships, Austria, Italy, Holland, Belgium and France being the other competing nations. The English team was: Alderson (Racers), English (Terriers); Shepherd (Lions), Doug Young (Racers), Alan Smith (Streatham) Clive Millard (Streatham Royals), Murray (Lions) (captain), Bobby Thompson, Soffe and Ravenscroft (all Terriers) O'Brien (Brighton Tigers) Knight (Sussex), Fresher (Rangers) and Gardner (Streatham) as forwards.

Vern Greger, defenceman with Streatham and Fife Flyers, lined-up with the new Edinburgn Royals, coached by Alec Archer.

There were two extraordinary happenings in 1952–53. On 4 December 1952, HRH The Duke of Edinburgh attended an ice hockey match at Wembley in which the Lions were beaten 2–1 by an All Star team chosen by 'Bob' Giddens and myself at the request of Sir Arthur Elvin. Also, the Murrayfield Ice Rink finally opened with 'Sandy' Archer as General Manager, and a new team, Edinburgh Royals, in the Scottish League.

In addition, the World and European Championships took on a different complexion with an A Group and a B Group. There were only four entries for the senior group – Sweden, Czechoslovakia, Switzerland (A) and Germany. Sweden were Champions, Czechoslovakia being withdrawn after the death of President Gottwald. Great Britain entered a team in the B Group with Johnny Murray as player-coach. The team did well, beating Switzerland (B), Holland, France and Austria and narrowly losing the decisive game to Italy 3–2 after a tremendous fight back from 3–0 down.

The team could well have won the Championship had it not been for some selection and administration blunders. In trying to keep everyone happy, Kenny Barnes, who had played with Streatham and Wembley Lions, was omitted in favour of poorer players; Yves Crenn, of Perth Black Hawks, was chosen, although he had a French passport and was barred from the competition on his arrival in Switzerland; and Wembley Lions refused to release Roy Shepherd.

'Bobby' Giddens urged 'Bunny' Ahearne not to send the squad without a team manager and suggested me, as I had previous experience of taking BIHA and other teams abroad. Moreover, Johnny Murray and I got along well together. 'Bunny' said the BIHA could not afford the extra expense. With hindsight it was a costly decision. It was a complete waste of money to take the unqualified Crenn and if there had been a team manager he would certainly not have travelled, one of the first duties of any competent manager being to check all the travel documents. A manager would also have allowed Murray to concentrate on the playing side, undistracted by other problems.

'If' is the biggest little word in the English language, but if Barnes had gone instead of Crenn and if Wembley had released Roy Shepherd, who knows what might have happened? Just the same, nothing should detract from an excellent performance by Great Britain, the more so since a number of the 'Italians' were Canadians holding Italian passports.

The British team was: English (Wembley Terriers) in goal; Spence (Perth Panthers), Bobby Thompson (Wembley Terriers), Cartwright (Durham Wasps), Bell (Durham Wasps) on defence; O'Brien (Southampton Vikings), Soffe (Wembley Terriers), Brennan (Glasgow Mohawks), Crenn (Perth Black Hawks), McCrae (Ayr Raiders), Ferguson (Glasgow Mohawks), Crawford (Glasgow Mohawks), Mudd (Grimsby Red Wings) and Murray (Wembley Terriers) (player-coach) as forwards. McCrae and Ferguson did especially well, but the general consensus was that Bill Crawford was top man on the team.

Streatham were England's Team of the Year after a tremendous tussle for the League Championship with Harringay and Brighton. What a team they had: Betker in the nets and in front of him four big hustling defencemen – Art Hodgins and Bill Winemaster, Fred Dunsmore and Vic Fildes. The six regular forwards were Don and Gordie Callaghan, Andre Charest, Ray

Goalmouth tussle in a match between Brighton Tigers and Harringay Racers. Brighton's fiery winger Freddie Sutherland (No. 6) fights for the puck.

Maisoneuve, Vic Kreklewetz and former Scottish star, Stu Robertson who, with Kreklewetz, provided the main scoring punch.

Streatham's other imports faltered for one reason or another. Hy Beatty was unlucky in suffering a broken ankle after playing 27 games for 33 points, but Appleton and Vallieres did not come up to expectations. Vallieres was homesick and returned to Canada; Appleton spent most of the season with the Swiss club, Davos. English boys Kenny Barnes, who played 38 games, and Kenny Gardner filled in, and 25-year-old Torontonian Harry Boyd, former Earls Court Ranger who quit the League for university and had starred in the previous inter-Varsity match, also turned out a few times.

There was a big storm one night at Streatham when a goal scored by Joe Shack as the final whistle went was hotly disputed. It might have cost Streatham the title, but Brighton obligingly put paid to Harringay's chances.

Wembley defenceman 'Sonny' Rost was inducted into the Hall of Fame. He was 42 years of age and still playing. He reminisced with me: 'I'll be 42 come March and as far back as I can remember I've been playing hockey. For 21 of those 42 years I've been happy and proud to wear a Wembley uniform. I'm not saying that hockey or any other sport is necessarily the best life for lads with lots of ambition. You've got to really like

The team that gave 'Sonny' Rost the biggest thrills of his hockey career, the 1948–49 Wembley Monarchs, winners of the Autumn Cup and International Tournament. 'Sonny' here receives the International Tournament trophy from Philip Vassar Hunter, BIHA President. Left to right: Les Anning, Alec 'Sandy' Archer (coach), Roy Thompson, Vassar Hunter, Mauno 'Kid' Kauppi, Rost, 'Red' Kurz, George Beach, Frank Trottier, 'Stubby' Mason, Don Thomson, Freddie Sutherland, Jean-Paul Lafortune, 'Mac' MacLachlan.

the game, and you don't play as long as I have unless you do.

'When you love a game, money isn't all that important. I remember during the war when Mr Bourke used to stage Service games down at Brighton, we would travel down there and play for about thirty shillings a game and it would cost us about £5 each.

'For a kid fresh out of Winnipeg, coming to play ice hockey at the Empire Pool when it opened in 1934 was like some fantastic dream come true.

'Over the years I've played with teams labelled Lions, Canadians, Monarchs and All Stars, but if you asked me to state a preference then I must admit that I enjoyed best the years I played with Monarchs. It was one of the biggest thrills of my life when in 1948–49 Monarchs captured the Autumn Cup and also took International Tournament honours against tip-top

The best-looking goalie Wembley ever had: Diana Dors takes time off from making *A Boy, A Girl and A Bike* to guard the nets against 'Sonny' Rost and 'Kid' Kauppi.

opposition which included Racing Club de Paris. We had a fine team that year. Remember the names? 'Stubby' Mason in the nets; Don Thomson, Roy Thompson, 'Red' Kurz and myself on defence; 'Kid' Kauppi, Les Anning, Jean-Paul Lafortune, George Beach, Freddie Sutherland, 'Mac' MacLachlan and Frank Trottier up-front.

'The following season we were always the bridesmaids but never the bride. We finished as runners-up in the National League, the Autumn Cup and the National Tournament. That was a grand team too: Mason; Ferens, Kurz, Winemaster,

Gawthrop; Prete, Lafortune, Beach, Dunkelman, Kauppi, Stay, Steele, Davidson, Lynn.

'But the outstanding memory was the night we beat the great Harringay Racers *by a cricket score* after losing to them the previous night at Harringay. That was the night it was so foggy that many supporters slept in the rink rather than try and make the journey home. Racers were top of the League and had a really powerful team: Lorne Lussier in the nets; Campbell and Linton on defence; Kennedy, Payette, Gawthrop, Ricard, Melnyk, Colvin up-front. Don Stay scored nine points and 'Stubby' Mason got his first shut-out in England, and we beat them 15–0.

'Mason was one of the outstanding characters in my hockey recollections. Once, when Monarchs were playing in Switzerland, he skated over to the barrier, snatched a policeman's hat and went back to his goal wearing it. The policeman was trying to climb the barrier to recover his headgear and the rest of us were so helpless with laughter we couldn't get on with the game.

'But most goalies are characters. Mason was the funniest I recall, but 'Turkey' Harnedy, who played in goal for Richmond many years ago, was another. 'Turkey' was absolutely unpredictable. Art Child, who minded the nets for both Lions and Monarchs and is now a Canadian Member of Parliament, also had his moments. Once he swore that he would never shave until he got a shut-out. I remember his beard was at least two inches long before it came off. Just between ourselves I think he cheated anyway.

'One of the best I ever played against was Joe Beaton. Joe was a centreman with Richmond and Harringay before the war and afterwards he played at Wembley. He always had his head up and was a real smart playmaker and scorer. I still see him watching the games, although these days he's in business for himself.

'You won't see many better left-wingers than Albert Lemay, who played with his brother Tony for Lions before the war. In fact, if I were picking a team, this would be my starting line-up, assuming all were at their peak: goal – Jimmy Foster (Richmond and Harringay); defence – Len Burrage (Harringay) and Frank Currie (Richmond, Harringay and Earls Court); centre – Joe Beaton (Richmond, Harringay and Wembley); right-wing – Bert Peer (Harringay); left-wing – Bert Lemay (Wembley).

'To my knowledge, Currie is the only one still connected with hockey and he coaches Calgary in the professional Western Hockey League.

'You may say that these players all made their name and fame in pre-war days. Well, there's a simple reason for that. In those days you could pick up the transatlantic phone and get a fellow like Hugh Farquharson, who led the Quebec Senior League scoring. Nowadays it would be financially impossible to get the top marksman from such a league.

'At that time New York Rovers were offering a player $25 a week, while over here they were paying $50. Conditions were bad in Canada and fellows were glad to cross the ocean. Now it's different. The $60 we pay doesn't stack up too well against the big money men can earn in very ordinary jobs in Canada and the States, even though the cost of living is not so high here. As a result the players we get here are the fellows who firstly love to play hockey for its own sake and secondly have the urge to see a bit of the world.

'But you'll always get guys who love to play the game. Fellows like Sid Abel, former captain of Detroit Red Wings. Sid was as big as they come, a fellow who ranked with the all-time greats. Yet when he was stationed over here he turned out for Wembley Lions without shinguards and with gloves a size too small. He didn't care. To him it was hockey, the greatest game on earth.

'I don't want to dwell on the old days. The post-war era has seen many good players. In fact, fellows like Chick Zamick, Kenny Booth, 'Kid' Kauppi and George Beach could rank with the best of them. It's a pleasure still to be playing with such grand guys. Hockey has always been a pleasure to me, and it's been good to me. Only one serious injury — when I cracked a collar-bone and broke three ribs at Brighton — and lots of happy memories, including the time when my brother Wally played over here with Wembley and Southampton Vikings.

'Yes, I'm just a bit of a Cockney after 21 years. Settled down, married, three children (John 12, Diane 8 and Pauline 5). Retire? Well, let's wait and see shall we?'

Thus 'Sonny' Rost back in 1953. He did not, in fact, retire for another ten years, long enough to line-up in the same match with son John, a modern All Star defenceman, and thus beat the great NHL star Gordie Howe to such a grand moment. John followed his father as a player and a coach and went on to become a member of the BIHA Council. 'Sonny's' grandson, Warren, has since made his début on Wembley ice.

Former Durham captain Pete ('Jonka') Johnson, like Gordie Howe, had the pleasure of two sons playing on the same team. Steve and Anthony Johnson are among the best of the present crop of British born-and-bred players.

The Rosts and the Johnsons are but two of the many families

in British hockey, among them the Hands and Lovells of Murrayfield, the Kewards of Nottingham, the Hunters at Peterborough, the Campbells of Durham and the Freshers, father and son.

Back in the year when 'Sonny' Rost made the Hall of Fame, Ayr Raiders were undisputed champions in Scotland, with Al Holliday again in the nets and a sound defence quartet of Herb Kewley (captain), Ray Dinardo, Gar Vasey and Scots-born Lawson Neil. André Girard was player-coach and he again had Ernie Domenico patrolling a wing, and Ernie, with 119 points, headed the season's scoring table. Girard himself was sixth in the list and these two carried the forward burden, the only other Ayr players in the top twenty-five being Ray Cazeau (ninth) and Jean Tremblay (twenty-second).

It was fitting that two such good teams as Raiders and Streatham should be Britain's best in this particular season, because 'the winds of change' were not blowing only in Africa . . .

9 ICING

The 1953—54 season was a climactic one in the story of British ice hockey. On the surface it was another good season with Nottingham Panthers, led by Les Strongman, pipping the favourites, Streatham, for the English National League title by one point, and Falkirk Lions once again coming through to take a sizzling Scottish play-off series defeating Perth Panthers after Paisley Pirates had finished top of the regular schedule by fourteen points.

Behind the scenes there were rumblings. Ice shows, pantomimes and circuses at the three big London arenas had disrupted schedules for some time, and Harringay and Wembley had cut down to one team apiece. In 1953 Empress Hall dropped out altogether, leaving England with five senior clubs — Nottingham, Streatham, Harringay, Wembley and Brighton. Scotland had seven at this time, and backroom discussions led to a decision to combine the two circuits in one big British League in 1954—55.

In theory this was a great idea, welcomed by many people — management, players and spectators. Others were not so sanguine about the prospect, and William Warman, Chairman of Streatham, voiced their fears when he said the new loop would give much-needed variety but would add about £100 per week to travelling costs — and in those days you could get four or five good hockey players for that. He pointed out the intolerable burden of Entertainment Tax and the high cost of Canadian players. The game had forced itself into a corner — it was no good getting less expensive players because a public reared on good-class hockey would not accept a lowering of standards. He also pointed out that small rinks like Streatham were at a great disadvantage compared with giant arenas such as Harringay and Wembley.

Not that all was prosperous with the larger rinks. Ice hockey, said Harringay, paid its way but it did not make enough money to support the arena all the year round. At the time the rates alone on Harringay Arena were £1,000. So it was necessary to try rodeos, circuses, roller speedway and even revivalist meetings in a bid to find other activities which could pay their way.

To try and keep the public informed about these problems, we at *Ice Hockey World* put some financial questions to the rinks and this is what we came up with in essence:

The average rink could accommodate between 3,000 and

4,000 spectators (there were some much bigger and one or two lower) and the average gate was about £770. Entertainment Tax swallowed £160 of this. Transport of Canadian players broken down into a weekly cost over a 33-week season came to £33 10s. A weekly players' wage bill was £212; equipment cost £36 10s. per week. If William Warman's calculations were correct (and he was head of an accountancy firm) British League travel would cost another £100, leaving a balance of £228. Out of this had to come rates, maintenance of the rink, wages of managerial, office and maintenance staff, printing and advertising. There could not have been much left in the kitty, and these calculations were based upon nearly full houses. How full would they be for British League matches?

The answer to that question was still a season away as Les Strongman received the League trophy from hockey immortal Carl Erhardt.

The last English National League champions before the amalgamation were: Jack Siemon (goal); Lorne Smith, Gerry Watson; Bill Allen, Doug Wilson (defence); Chick Zamick, George Horb, Les Strongman (captain); Bill Ringer, Bill Maslanko, Ernie Dougherty (forwards). Sam Strachan, Davie Ritchie, Brian Beardsley, Ron Larter, Cam Miller and Doug Hamilton also played some games. On the night they received the trophy they were beaten in an exhibition match by *Ice Hockey World* All Stars.

George McNeil, once again Scotland's most successful coach, gave a 16-year-old local boy, 'Red' Imrie, a chance in the Falkirk line-up. *Ice Hockey World* Scottish columnist Eddie Blane wrote, 'I've never seen a teenager with so much potential.' In the coming years Imrie would be a bright star in the hockey firmament, eventually a coach and then a television commentator. The tragedy is that in what should have been his prime years the sport was in the doldrums.

1954 was a sad season on some personal fronts. Joe Shack suffered an eye injury in Sweden and virtually bowed out of the game. 'Duke' Macdonald had his final year as coach at Harringay and the old St Louis Flyer went out gallantly, donning skates and uniform in an emergency despite his age. The hero of Brighton, Bobby Lee, hung up his skates 18 years and 472 goals after making his English National League début.

The biggest shock, however, was reserved for Canada, beaten by the Russians in the World Championship in which Great Britain did not take part. The CAHA – rightly – bore the blame. They sent an unknown team, Toronto Lyndhursts, to do battle with Europe's best, and although their coach realised they

needed reinforcing and four players, including former Brighton and Earls Court defenceman Tommy Jamieson, were flown over it was not enough. Before the four recruits arrived a combined Wembley-Harringay team had beaten Lyndhursts 11–2.

On the intermediate front Wembley Terriers won the Southern League, Durham the Northern and Blackpool the Midland. 'Icy' Smith got permission to proceed with a new rink at Whitley Bay, and the British firm which built Dundee, Kirkcaldy and Dunfermline built the world's first ice rink in a desert – at Baghdad.

In the autumn the British League was launched to a flurry of trumpets. It comprised twelve teams. Streatham had carried out their threat to withdraw, but Dunfermline, which had not

First-ever British League Champions, Harringay Racers, left to right: standing – Harry Aldridge (trainer), Bill Winemaster, Art Hodgins, Bill Glennie (player-coach), Les Lilley, Gene Miller, Rupe Fresher, 'Moose' Smith; kneeling – Vic Kreklewetz, 'Nipper' Millard, Al Buchholz, Ray Maisoneuve, Fred Denny.

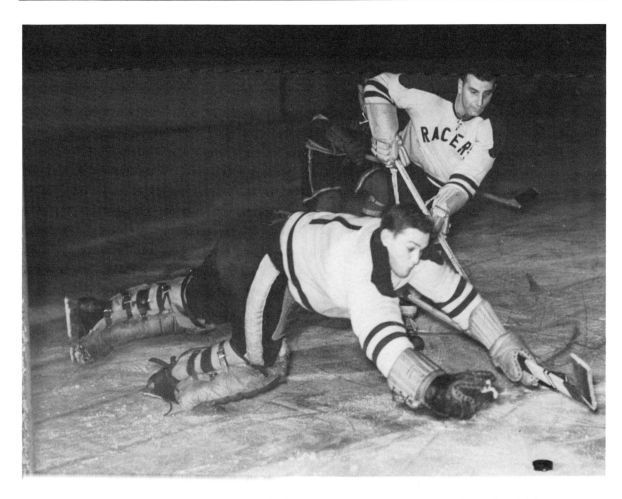

Former Brighton goalie, Al Buchholz, and ex-Streatham wingers, Vic Kreklewetz, unite in the cause of defending Harringay's goal

operated the previous season, returned to the fold. However, after completing the Autumn Cup schedule in which they won only two matches, Vikings played only eleven League games before folding, their results being expunged from the records.

Despite surprisingly good performances from Falkirk and Paisley, Harringay Racers were undoubtedly the Team of the Year, winning both the League and the Cup. Player-coach Bill Glennie was Player of the Year; defencemen Art Hodgins and Bill Winemaster together with right-winger Fred Denny were voted on to the All Star A team, along with trainer Harry Aldridge; and centre Gene Miller and left-winger Ray Maisoneuve made the B team. Vic Kreklewetz was voted outstanding utility man, and Les Lilley Rookie of the Year. English players Rupe Fresher and Clive Millard did well, and when goalie Al Buchholz was injured another English player, the appropriately-named Gordon English, shut-out Perth Panthers.

Glennie, William John Glennie to give him his full name, is one of those rare players who introduced a new move into the game – and one which gave rise to a great deal of controversy. In a nutshell, he would circle behind his own defencemen and an opponent, congratulating himself on breaking through, would run into the father-and-mother of a bodycheck from Bill. In Scotland, referees ruled him out of order whenever he attempted it, but gradually people got used to the idea and it was accepted as legal. Few people outside his own team knew that Bill was a first-class skate-grinder, and even when he was player-coach and manager of Racers none of the team would let anyone else touch their skates. No one could put an edge on the blades like William John Glennie.

Nottingham, with substantially their title-winning team of the previous season plus Pat Cooney and George Chin, the first but not the last Chinaman to play in the League, came close to winning again. Zamick, again leading scorer, and Strongman, made All Star A; Siemon, Watson and Trainer Charlie Cragg the B team. Ayr had the first coloured player in a British club, Alf Lewsey, a fine player who made All Star B.

Keith Kewley's Paisley Pirates were a big surprise, relying heavily as they did on Scots-born players. Tiny Syme, considered to be the poorer player of the Syme brothers and also one with a tendency to temper, was given the job of captain and reacted to the responsibility by turning in his best season ever, teamed with another Scot, Joe Brown. Bill Crawford and Billy Brennan, two more Scots, did well in attack. With All Star A goalie, Ed Lochhead, Scottish Rookie of the Year Tommy Lemon, and two very good forwards in Paul Provost and George Samolenko, Pirates were a very pleasing team. At the time of writing, Provost is still playing Old Timers' hockey in Canada.

Wembley Terriers, coached by Johnny Murray, continued their triumphant way in intermediate circles winning both Southern and Northern competitions, Grimsby taking the Midland. Southampton Vikings had a good year and the rink staged an international, England v. USA.

Nottingham beat the Swedish national team to retain for Britain the Ahearne Trophy, which had been won the two previous seasons by Harringay, and Canada obtained sweet revenge by regaining the World Championship, beating Russia 5–0 in the process. Canada was represented by Allan Cup Champions, Penticton Vees. Several of them, including player-coach Grant Warwick, an all-time great with New York

Rangers, and his brother Bill, were former professionals. The sad thing is that in victory they made no friends. They were the most boorish, unsociable and aggressive team Canada has ever sent to Europe. They criticised British and European hockey and gave no credit at all to Harringay Racers who beat them 5–3. Before the match they treated both Harringay officials and players like dirt, not to mention the Press. It was not only the British who were unimpressed with Canada's attitude. A Canadian publication commented, 'You would have thought Penticton had won the Holy Grail instead of just another hockey match.'

Racers exacted satisfaction in the best way possible – on the ice. The Harringay scorers were Maisoneuve (2), Miller, Barr and Kreklewetz; Dick Warwick, Grant Warwick and McAvoy replying for Canada. It was Bill Glennie's birthday and he laid on the passes for two of the goals. Brighton's Alf Harvey, formerly of Earls Court, guested on the Harringay defence and played an outstanding game.

Another name disappeared from the scene during the off-season. Paul Herbert, general manager of Wembley Empire Pool for eighteen years, died aged 51. He had been the power behind many great Wembley teams.

The much-needed variety which the British League was to supply lasted only one season, and 1955–56 saw the League reduced to five teams – Harringay, Wembley, Brighton, Nottingham and Paisley. Travelling and hotel costs, variable attendances and disparity in playing strengths caused the other rinks to pull out.

Most of the Scottish rinks took part in the Scottish Amateur League, but unfortunately an apparent backlash in official circles kept out players who could have helped greatly by practical example. A typical example was ace goaltender Al Holliday, who was allowed to coach Ayr Raiders but not permitted to play.

In the British League, Chick Zamick got his 600th goal (against Paisley) and Nottingham, coached by the selfsame Zamick, deservedly won the title.

Brighton Tigers included several stars from Scottish clubs including 'Red' Kurz, Gar Vasey and Syd Arnold, but many others, out of a job by virtue of the collapse of their clubs, found player-coach berths in Switzerland and elsewhere on the Continent. Johnny Oxley was appointed player-coach at Brighton, the first British born-and-bred player to be made coach of a senior team.

Gib Hutchinson came out of a three-year retirement, aged 41, to help Brighton against USA, because Brighton's regular goalie was injured. The old maestro made some great saves, held off power plays and fired long passes out to his forwards. Later on he again deputised in the League. Like good brandy, Hutch certainly matured with the years.

The United States were only one of several foreign teams to spice the domestic season, the Swedes, Czechs and Russians also visiting.

The Russians won the Olympic, World and European titles, and the Canadian Amateur Hockey Association, doubtless with judgement clouded by Penticton's victory, showed that they hadn't learned anything from the previous season. They did send a good team over, Kitchener-Waterloo Flying Dutchmen, twice Allan Cup winners, and coached by former Boston great (and wartime Durham idol) Bobby Bauer. 'Our best in thirty-four years,' glibly pronounced CAHA Secretary, George Dudley, thus blandly dismissing Winnipeg Monarchs, Trail Smoke Eaters and the controversial Penticton Vees.

Although Keith Woodall, former Streatham netman, played well, the Russians defeated Canada 2−0 and it was USA, coached by ex-Chicago Black Hawk Johnny Mariucci, who finished runners-up. The tough Mariucci, one of the few Americans in the NHL in his time, started a riot when he played at Paisley during the USA tour of Britain, but that's another story.

On the home front Southampton Vikings again had a good year, winning the BIHA Cup by defeating Glasgow Mohawks. They had a number of players with senior experience and in February 1956 scored 23 goals against Liverpool. The same month Ayr Raiders withdrew from the Scottish Amateur League and there was talk that the seaside rink would revert to senior hockey the next season.

In March there was a boost for the game when the first commercial television coverage was beamed from Nottingham, with Alan Weeks handling the commentary. Wembley Lions beat the League leaders Panthers 8−3.

Alas, however, British ice hockey was destined to decline. The British League would expire in 1960 and only four teams would be ever-present during its six years of life − Nottingham, Paisley, Wembley and Brighton. Wembley were champions in 1957, Brighton in 1958, Paisley in 1959 and Streatham, back in the fold, in 1959−60. In the same period, Brighton twice won the Autumn Cup, Wembley once and Streatham once. Ironically, as British big-time hockey was about to breathe its last, in 1959 New York Rangers and Boston Bruins played a couple of games here at the beginning of a European tour. There was also one tremendous victory for fans to recall and savour in the bleak years ahead – the night Brighton Tigers became the first British team to beat the all-conquering Russian squad.

Early in December 1957 the Russians arrived to play matches against Harringay Racers, Brighton Tigers and Paisley Pirates. On Wednesday 4 December in a rink only two-thirds full due to fog, Racers, proud of their reputation against overseas visitors, halted the Russian trail of success by battling them to a 3–3 tie.

Former Ayr goalie Al Holliday was in sparkling form in the Harringay nets, and it was cruel luck when the Russians went ahead. Johnny Carlyle, the Scot who captained Racers, dropped his stick, bent down to pick it up and a shot going wide hit him and was deflected past Holliday.

Racers fought back in the second period, defenceman Hall firing three hard shots, the third of which went in the net and brought the scores level. Then, with another Racer rearguard, Johnston, in the penalty-box, player-coach Bill Glennie and Marshall Key, another product of Scottish hockey, set about killing off the penalty. They did it in such deft fashion that before the Russians knew what was happening, Key had slipped the puck to Glennie and the tall wingman had scored. Racers were flying now and Woods made it 3–1.

The home team tired in the third period and the Russians tallied twice to level the scores, a clear illustration of the advantage of three forward lines over two.

The Harringay team which put up such a good fight was: Holliday; Hall, Carlyle; Johnston, McRae; Key, Glennie, Seguin; Dorohoy, Woods, Chacalias; McKay.

No one expected Brighton to go one better the following night by beating the Russians, but that's just what the Tigers did. And they beat them well, by a 6–3 score. Many thought it the most exciting match they had ever seen.

The stadium was packed to see the Russians take a 3–0 stranglehold on the game. Undeterred, Tigers pulled two back in the second period and fired four more home in the third.

The official referees, Bill Lewthwaite and Les Pearson, were delayed by fog, so Johnny Flynn handled the first period on his own. That period could be summed up simply – Russia versus Tony Parisi, the Brighton goalie. The brilliant Tony had 22 shots fired at him and he was magic. Two beat him, but he could not be faulted, whilst at the other end the Russian netman Litovko faced only five shots.

Five minutes into the second period and Russia went further in front, but Tigers were fighting back and Tommy Rendall emerged from a tangle of Russian defenders to score Brighton's first. Three minutes from the end of the period former Falkirk Lion Ron Flinn broke away, chased desperately by a lone Russian. Flinn skated three-quarters the length of the rink, kept his head and flicked the puck to the far corner of the net.

The final period was fantastic. Play was end-to-end; there were near misses galore; and through it all the never-say-die Tigers steamed in for four goals and a mighty triumph.

The team that won itself a slice of immortality that night was Tony Parisi (goal); 'Red' Kurz, Ross Kelly and Art Hodgins (defence); Ron Flinn, Tom Rendall, Lloyd Orris; Hemmerling, Fred Denny, Joe Connors; Morrison (forwards).

The Russians went on to beat Paisley 4−1, but nothing could take away from Brighton's magnificent victory.

The mid-1950s were years of decision for many of us for whom hockey had been our life and our livelihood for so many years. One day Jack Elvin and I took an All Star team down to Southampton to play the local Vikings. Johnny Flynn, defence-men 'Red' Kurz and Roy Thompson and the legendary Joe Shack were in the party. We were all married men, all a little uncertain about the future, and on the way back to London we seriously discussed forming a team to tour Europe the next season. We would have a base − Roy had been asked to join a French club and bring some players with him − and under the influence of a beer or three it was agreed that Joe, Roy and I would make the necessary arrangements. It didn't work out as planned. 'Red' stayed in British hockey to lead Brighton to glory against the Russians, Joe took off into the television industry and Jack Elvin stayed with his photo-engraving business in London's West End.

As for me, I hung up my skates, picked up my typewriter and stepped off the Great Ice Way into a world where the sports were cricket, boxing, athletics and football, and later motor racing and rallying. The money was better and the cheques more regular. I didn't know it, but I wasn't finished with hockey.

Ice Hockey World, once selling 50,000 copies per week and stacked with national advertising, publishing a special Scottish edition and with a best-selling Annual, had nosedived with the sport. 'Bob' Giddens and I had made reluctant economies, chopped staff and tightened the belts. I had a wife to consider, so had 'Bob'. It seemed possible to me that as long as there was some sort of hockey *Ice Hockey World* might survive as a one-man firm. To support two of us and our families just was not possible. For some time we had been surviving by virtue of a half-hour sports programme which we produced for Canadian radio.

'Bob' tried to persuade me to stay. With a deep regret I slid the case on my trusty typewriter, took a last look at the office which had been home from home for so long, shook hands with 'The Beaver' as he was known to staff in our more prosperous days and walked around the corner to a sports desk in Fleet Street.

It was easier to keep in touch with the sport than one would have thought. 'Red' Stapleford, Freddie Dunkelman and Jack Elvin all had offices within half a mile or so. 'Chick' Zamick, down from Nottingham, would drop in to discuss plans for his squash club. Ex-Harringay Hornet and senior referee Jimmy Creed came by when over from Baltimore which he now called home. Gerry Heffernan was a regular visitor from his home in Montreal, as was Henry Hayes. One night we had a reunion in a pub at Wembley – 'Lou' Bates, 'Sonny' Rost, Gerry Heffernan, Jake Brunning, Joe Shack, Jack Elvin. Charles Riccono, Italian newspaperman based in London, the man who recruited Mike Daski, Kenny Westman, Ray Dinardo and others for the Milano Red-and-Black Devils, bobbed up everywhere, and so did big Belgian enthusiast and journalist Maurice Simon. 'Red' Kurz, married to a London girl, came by and talked about settling permanently in East Anglia. Hockey was never far away . . .

'Bobby' Giddens never lived to see the revival of the game to which he had devoted his life. He died in 1962 after a long and painful illness, only 56 years of age. Journalism can be a tough taskmaster, and I was away on assignment at the time of his funeral so my wife was there in my stead. 'The Beaver' would have understood. To him the job always came first. I was with him just a short time before he died, and he still believed that one day hockey would make a come-back.

It was an honour and a privilege to nominate 'Bobby' Giddens for British hockey's Hall of Fame when it was revived by the British Ice Hockey Writers' Association in 1985–86. Howard Bass, a distinguished contributor to *Ice Hockey World*, received the scroll on our behalf, and Bob's widow Margaret and their two sons, Bobby Jnr and Gary, now have it as a prized possession. No man did more to earn it.

10 LIGHT BLUE, DARK BLUE

Over the years the annual University Boat Race has attracted thousands of spectators and millions more through the medium of television, many of whom have never been to Oxford, Cambridge or any other university and the majority of whom have never rowed a boat of any description. Ice hockey has never enjoyed the same status as the Boat Race, either at the universities themselves or in the eyes of the public. Yet no history of British ice hockey can ignore the part played by Varsity puck-chasers, especially in the formative years of the game.

In the March 1985 issue of *Ice Hockey World* I wrote the following; may it serve as a tribute to the good hockey players and the bad, the serious ones and the jokers, the administrators and the beer-drinkers, in fact all of those who have contributed to the rich diverse pattern of ice hockey as played in our nobler seats of learning.

'You're kidding,' I said to Fred Meredith, President of the British Ice Hockey Association and former Cambridge University goalminder.

Cambridge University in action against Nottingham Panthers in 1982. Nottingham's Tim Peacock is the man getting 'the treatment' from Light Blue defenders.

'I kid you not,' said Fred, 'the first ice hockey match between Cambridge and Oxford Universities was played at St Moritz in 1885 and I regret to report that Oxford won 6–0. The match is recorded in the files of both universities and has now been recognised by the International Ice Hockey Federation not only as the first Varsity match but also as the first ice hockey match outside Canada. To commemorate this the BIHA is presenting an official plaque to both universities.'

The centenary of the Battle of the Blues was a case of high jinks all round. One celebration dinner was held in Canada, since over the years the majority of players on both teams have been Canadian-born with a sprinkling of Americans and others amongst the native sons. A second dinner was held in Britain, but such was the enthusiasm that some fifty former players crossed the Atlantic for a second go at the turtle consommé and the sole à la Provence – or was it bangers and mash? Amongst them were some great British players of yester-year, including Carl Erhardt and 'Bibo' de Marwicz. With Ernie Ramus, Ralph Couldrey and Baron 'Dickie' von Trauttenberg, they were pillars of the Streatham team in the pre-war National League.

Erhardt, who learned his hockey on the Continent, was a formidable defenceman who captained Streatham even when top-class Canadians appeared in the League. His greatest triumph was leading the Great Britain team which won the Olympic, World and European Championships in 1936. Von Trauttenberg, another university player, was also good enough to be a regular on the Streatham defence and captained his native country, Austria, in international competition.

Coupled with these celebrations was the 67th Varsity match, played at Peterborough on 3 March 1985.

Did Cambridge play Oxford 100 years ago? They probably did. Was it ice hockey? Probably not as we know it, but then the origins of every sport are obscure and all the arguments over the first ice hockey matches boil down to the definition of 'ice hockey'. In most of those early games, the number of players varied and so did the rules. Shinty, bandy and field hockey were all converted to games on ice, and equipment from all these games was used, plus balls and all sorts of objects doing duty for what we now call a puck. We shall probably never know what form of the game was played in St Moritz in 1885 since the official records show merely that it was played and the result.

It is generally believed, however, that the first ice hockey clubs were not formed at the universities until around 1900. In that year, at the instigation of Jack Cawthra, a Canadian from Toronto who played the game in his native city as early as 1889,

Varsity hockey player Roger Mawditt went on to play for Peterborough Pirates, Brighton Royals and become a Peterborough director.

Can you see tough defender Robin Andrew as a figure skater? The durable and much-travelled international has played for Aviemore, Streatham, Southampton, Oxford and Nottingham amongst others, and is one of the soundest rearguards in modern hockey.

Cambridge met Oxford at Princes Club, London. They played five-a-side and Oxford won 7–6.

Cawthra, captain of Cambridge, was easily the best man on the ice. He was a remarkable sportsman who gained a full Blue for athletics and half Blues for lacrosse and speed-skating. He played for England at lacrosse and also played for England in the International Ice Hockey League Championship at St Moritz in 1913. He was runner-up in the Canadian figure-skating championships in 1908. Somehow I can't see Ron Plumb, Cal Land, Pete Johnson and Robin Andrews as figure-skaters. (But you never know; one season Hazen McAndrew, Jack Keating and Gerry Heffernan learned to ice *dance*.)

The first English Ice Hockey League was formed in 1903, and Cambridge entered but Oxford did not. The Light Blues finished fifth and last, winning only one of their eight matches.

Unless you count an eleven-a-side bandy match at Blenheim Palace, the Varsity match did not take place again after 1901 until Sir Henry Lunn revived it in 1909 when Oxford beat Cambridge 5–3 at Wengen, Switzerland.

During most of this period Rhodes Scholars at Oxford played as Oxford Canadians and they were good enough to beat the international teams of Switzerland, Germany and Belgium. However, the Canadians were left out of the Varsity matches, which were consequently of a low standard. After 1913 it was decided to allow at least two North Americans to play for each side, but this rule could not be carried out until the series resumed in 1920 after the First World War.

The Oxford University Ice Hockey Club was formed on a proper basis in 1921, and for the next three seasons Oxford enjoyed their greatest successes. It was largely due to the captain and goalminder, a Canadian named Ken Taylor. At Murren on 22 December 1921 Oxford defeated Cambridge 27–0. That Oxford team made history, for it was never beaten. On a tour of Switzerland it beat the Swiss National team 9–0 and went on to wallop Davos and St Moritz by even bigger margins, scoring 87 goals against two from their opponents.

Cambridge had a much better side the following season, but even so were beaten 7–1 by the all-conquering Dark Blues who also defeated the German national team in Berlin and scored victories over Paris, Davos and the British Army's All-Canadian squad.

Taylor was no longer available in 1923, but enough of his inspiration lingered on for Oxford to beat Cambridge 3–0 before embarking on another winning tour. Neville Melland was at Oxford around this time and he later did well in English hockey with Manchester and the highly capable Richmond Hawks.

By 1927 it was Cambridge's turn to have a captain and goalminder Murray Forbes who ran the team properly. They beat Oxford 3–0, the first time the Light Blues had won since 1913. Forbes was chosen for England v. Belgium. Cambridge reached the semi-finals of the Spengler Cup and won nine of their other twelve matches.

'Bibo' de Marwicz appeared for Cambridge in 1928 (they beat Oxford 1–0) and was one of three Cambridge players invited to join the British Olympic team.

Baron von Trauttenberg was captain of Cambridge in 1930–31, but Oxford, inspired by Larry Bonnycastle, the third of three fine brothers, won 5–1. With the opening of a rink at Oxford (not the present one), the Dark Blues had a permanent home for the first time and they proceeded to make the most of it. Herbie Little, Oxford's great goalminder, played for England, as did Fawcett, MacCullum and de Marwicz of Cambridge. Von Trauttenberg captained the Austrian team which won the European Championship.

In 1932 there was a packed house at Richmond when the Varsity match was played in England for the first time since 1901, Oxford winning 7–0. Oxford were League champions that year, winning all twelve of their matches. They also won the Spengler and Anspang Cups in Switzerland and drew with the touring Boston Olympics, who had previously beaten the English and French national teams. The same Oxford forward line played the entire game.

The Mayor of Oxford presented the team with gold medals for winning the League. The local paper advised Larry Bonnycastle that his speeches were not as good as his goals and they advised him to take up professional hockey instead of the legal profession. This great year in Dark Blue history was climaxed with a decision to award half Blues for ice hockey.

Oxford were League Champions again in 1933 and shared the Spengler and Hanseatic Cups with Prague.

The following season Oxford were third in the League. The face of hockey was changing and the Canadian undergraduates found themselves up against Grosvenor House Canadians and Queens, both teams loaded with Canadians and international players. Cambridge, now using Purley as a home rink, had an excellent new recruit in Canadian Army officer, Jimmy Carr, who later played with Wembley Canadians.

Both Universities dropped out of the League in 1934–35 neither having a home rink, Oxford's having closed. By 1936 both universities were based at Earls Court, but after the Second World War neither team had a permanent home, Richmond being their saviour. The standard of play was often very low, but there were some good and exciting games.

Now with a new Oxford rink and the Light Blues based at nearby Peterborough, let's hope for a big upsurge in university hockey.

The above article, and articles written by Martin Bronstein in the *Observer* and the *Toronto Globe & Mail*, brought a lot of correspondence, much of it from folk championing one place or another as the beginning of ice hockey. Bill Fitsell, of Kingston, Ontario, pointing out that his city was celebrating the centenary of the first game played in Kingston on Ash Wednesday 1886 between Queens University and the Royal Military College of Canada, demanded to know the names of the players in the 1885 Oxford and Cambridge match.

Perhaps the most interesting letter was from Hugh Whitney Morrison, of Thornhill, Ontario, who was a member of the Oxford Championship team of 1931–32. Fifty-three years on he gave the full line-up of that team:

Archie Humble (New Brunswick), 'Si' Leach (Dartmouth), Leland Watson (Minnesota), Herbie Little (Toronto) (goalie and co-captain), Larry Bonnycastle (Manitoba) (co-captain), 'Snooks' Gratias (Saskatchewan), James Coyne (Manitoba), John Babbitt (New Brunswick) and Morrison himself. All bar Leach were Rhodes Scholars and all bar Watson (an American) were Canadians. At the time Morrison wrote, all were alive except Babbitt and Watson.

Babbitt and Bonnycastle were one of the most dangerous duos in the history of Varsity hockey, as were Pitblado and an older Bonnycastle some years earlier. With a good defence and a man who was probably the best netminder in Britain at the time, it was little wonder that Oxford were champions. The second line, however, was not so good, and this has been the problem of Varsity sides over the years, a handful of good players and teams made up of anyone who could stand up on skates.

With teams tending to use more players, with hockey competition getting tougher in all nations and with universities putting more emphasis on learning to the exclusion of the sporty types, Oxford and Cambridge had many troubles after the Second World War, not least because some of their secretaries were too ambitious and embroiled the teams in tours against clubs too strong for them. Teams were not always well turned out, and once I saw a Varsity player poling himself along as if he was in a punt on the Cam.

According to Martin Bronstein, Oxford's netman in 1970 was Andy Rowan, a first-class wicket-keeper from South Africa. Unfortunately he could not skate and legend has it that they used to tie him to the goal-posts.

In recent years there have been changes for the better. University teams usually turn out looking the part of hockey players and usually have a squad all of whom can skate. With regular ice time available to them, Oxford and Cambridge may yet recapture some of their former glory.

11 POWER PLAY

London Lions skated again in the 1973–74 season in a courageous and experimental bid to bring big-time hockey back to Great Britain. These 'Londoners' originated from the United States and Canada, the man behind them being Bruce Norris, head of the Detroit Red Wing organisation. With the co-operation of 'Bunny' Ahearne, President of both the International Ice Hockey Federation and the British Ice Hockey Association, Norris and his associates, who included John Ziegler, now President of the National Hockey League, proposed playing a full season of matches against Europe's leading teams, both home and away.

Wembley provided home ice, and a very full fixture list was arranged involving playing 71 matches between 11 October 1973 and 31 March 1974, an average of a match every two and a half days. It was a mind-boggling schedule bearing in mind the time spent in travel to Sweden, Finland, Holland, Belgium, Luxembourg, Austria, West Germany, Switzerland and Czechoslovakia, as well as the home countries.

The ultimate aim was the formation of a European super-league, run on similar lines to the NHL but with all the major hockey nations of Europe taking part. Unfortunately, however,

The men who brought London Lions from Detroit to Wembley in a brave attempt to create a European super-league. Left to right: back row – Johnny Carlyle, Doug Barkley, Alan Weeks; front – Joe Besch, 'Bunny' Ahearne, Bruce Norris, John Ziegler.

the Europeans could not see their way to forming a league, so after the season ended London Lions were disbanded. Television commentator Alan Weeks, who was a director of the Lions, says now: 'It is possible that the idea was too far ahead of its time. It is possible that such a league would have been feasible ten years later.'

Certainly, no effort was spared to get the project off the ground. In addition to Alan Weeks, Johnny Carlyle, former Falkirk, Harringay and Great Britain player, was recruited as Scottish representative and a top-class professional coach, Doug Barkley, was in charge of the team.

Lions opened their campaign in Detroit where they defeated Toledo Hornets 1–0 prior to leaving for England. They played and won two matches at Wembley on 19 and 21 October against Austrian Internationals and then they were off on their first Continental trip. Amongst the many famous clubs they met during the season were Prague, Helsinki IFK, AIK Stockholm, Djurgarden, Dynamo Moscow, Spartak Moscow, Turku, and the Czech and West German national squads.

In the Ahearne Cup, held as usual in Sweden, they beat AIK Stockholm 3–1, Dynamo Moscow 2–1 and Sodertalje 6–4. They drew 5–5 with Regina Pats, the Canadian representatives, but lost 5–3 to Djurgarden and 6–1 to Leksand. Djurgarden, who lost only to Dynamo Moscow, were the Cup winners.

Lions did not confine their missionary work to the Continent. They defeated a Scottish Select 10–1 at Kirkcaldy, an International Select 12–1 at Dundee, and a North-East Select 15–6 at Billingham and 12–3 at Whitley Bay. Later in the season they beat Altrincham Aces 6–2 in a match played at Deeside.

The Wembley matches attracted many former Lion and Monarch fans and a whole host of celebrities, amongst them Lord Thomson of Fleet, former England football captain Bobby Moore (who used to watch hockey at Harringay), comedian Eric Morecambe, football manager Gordon Jago (whose wife June was once a Streatham supporter) and Arsenal goalkeeper now television commentator Bob Wilson. A supporters' club was formed, and Wembley's great centreman of yester-year, George Beach, accepted the office of Chairman.

Right-winger Earl Anderson was Lion's top goal-scorer and, together with captain Rick McCann and vice-captain Ulf Sterner, both centres, provided most of the scoring punch. First-choice goalie was Leif Holmqvist. In the Geneva Tournament, won by the Czech Under-23 team, London's Dennis 'Mighty Atom' Polonich was voted Most Valuable Player.

At the end of the season London Lions had won 53, lost 12,

Father v. son: John Rost (left) has the unique experience of playing for Brighton against Streatham and coming up against Dad. 'Still an awkward customer in his fifties,' smiled John.

Mike Madine, one of the stalwarts who kept British ice hockey alive in the 'twilight years'.

drawn 6 and scored 447 goals against 222. A valiant effort, but it did not do the trick — British hockey would have to seek salvation elsewhere.

It found it in the staunch efforts of a hard core of players and administrators, young, old and in-between, who gave freely of their time, money and effort to keep the game going in some form or another through the twilight years of the 1960s and 1970s to finally get their reward with the re-emergence of a British League in the 1980s.

Through the early 1960s serious competitive hockey was virtually non-existent in Britain although the BIHA, with a reservoir of home-grown talent developed in better times, val-iantly continued to send teams to the World and European

Championships in 1961, 1962, 1963 and 1966. In Colorado, USA, in 1962, the British squad was eighth in Pool A of the World Championship and sixth in the European, goalminder Derek Metcalfe (Durham) being named world No. 2. Until 1963 Britain was never out of the top ten.

Canada won the world title in 1961, Sweden in 1962 but after that, apart from the occasional take-over by the Czechs, the Russians had years of domination.

Britain did not return to the scene until 1971 and through the 1970s played only in Pool C, the third and last group of the Championships and – thus are the mighty fallen – were only once out of the cellar, in Barcelona in 1979. Britain's last appearance in the senior world competition was in 1981 in Peking – bottom again.

Hockey was kept going in the early 1960s largely in Scotland and the North of England, the long, slow and painful road back really starting in the 1966–67 season with the formation of a Northern League, followed by a Northern Autumn Cup and then in 1970–71 a Southern League.

From 1965 to 1980 the 'Icy' Smith Cup was regarded by most as emblematic of the British Championship.

Through two decades Edinburgh's Murrayfield Racers were Britain's outstanding team. Between 1966 and 1982 Racers won the Northern League seven times, Paisley Mohawks three and Dundee Rockets, Whitley Warriors and Fife Flyers twice apiece. Billingham Bombers, Glasgow Dynamos, Durham Wasps, Crowtree Chiefs, Edinburgh Royals, Whitley Bandits, Ayr Bruins, Aviemore Blackhawks, Perth Blackhawks and Paisley Vikings also competed at different times, but only Racers, Warriors, Flyers, Dynamos and Wasps stayed the pace through sixteen seasons.

Murrayfield's dominance extended to the 'Icy' Smith Cup. Between 1965 and 1980, Racers took the cup eight times against two for Fife Flyers and Whitley Warriors, and loners for Glasgow Dynamos, Paisley Mohawks and Ayr Bruins.

There was a similar story in the Northern Autumn Cup, launched in 1967 with Paisley Mohawks as winners and continued through to 1980 with a gap in 1969 and another in 1973. Whitley won in 1971, but that apart the trophy was virtually the exclusive property of Murrayfield and Fife, the former winning six times and the latter four.

1970 saw the formation of a Southern Ice Hockey Association and a Southern League with five teams based upon three rinks. By 1974 there were two Leagues, eleven teams and seven rinks. Two years later there were twenty-two teams utilising

One of modern hockey's greats and a member of the Hall of Fame: Roy Halpin, of Dundee Rockets, seen here in action against Murrayfield Racers.

twelve rinks. The Northern Ice Hockey Association was making similar progress. Six teams from six rinks in 1970 had grown to fifteen teams and eight rinks six years later, plus junior teams.

Crowtree (Sunderland) opened in 1978, the year Richmond returned to hockey. Bradford staged its first hockey in 1979 and Nottingham returned to the fold in 1980. Streatham had a million-pound face-lift and there were eighteen senior teams in England.

Sussex Senators were first champions of the Southern League, with Altrincham Aces as runners-up, but it was the durable George Beach, now playing for Wembley Vets, who headed the scoring lists some twenty-two years after he first came to Britain to play hockey. Sussex were champions again the following season and then it was Altrincham's turn. Streatham won four years in a row, before Solihull Barons took the title in 1978. Bristol Redwings, Blackpool Seagulls, Southampton Vikings, Avon Arrows, Liverpool Leopards, Oxford and Cambridge Universities, Grimsby Buffaloes, Deeside Dragons, Sheffield Lancers, London All Stars (Sobell Centre) and London Phoenix Flyers (Richmond) were others to take part.

The scoring champions in addition to Beach were Tom McMillan (Wembley Vets), Tony Whitehead (Wembley Vets), Ron Drennan (Altrincham Aces) and Richard Bacon (Streatham), twice. Between 1972 and 1975, Glynne Thomas (Wembley Vets and Streatham) was top goalie.

It sounds easier than it was. Clubs often had to beg ice time from their local rink or play all their matches away; and when they were allowed time it was often in the early hours of the morning or very late at night. In a way, it was a throw-back to Carl Erhardt's young days when the ice clubs charged high fees and preferred figure skaters to hockey players.

The durability of some of the players who kept hockey going in the twilight years was amazing. In 1976–77 an Old Timers squad included the following, most of whom had played in the old British National League: 'Fish' Robertson and Glynne Thomas (goal); Roy Shepherd, John Rost, 'Red' Imrie, Rupe Fresher, George Beach, Mike O'Brien (captain), Tony Whitehead, Roy Yates, John Cook, Kenny Flood and Mike Madine. Madine (ex-Wembley) and Yates (ex-Sussex) played together for Southampton and twenty years later were still playing together for Avon Arrows.

Many of the players and officials of that time were still active in the 1980s. These often unsung heroes are the main reason the game is fit and flourishing today. They include names like Allen Woodhead (Grimsby), Gordon Manuel (Aviemore), Frank

Dempster (Scottish IHA), Graham Nurse (Altrincham), Jackie Dryburgh (Kirkcaldy), Tom Shingle (Durham), Hep Tindale (Durham), Alfie Miller (Whitley), Sam Stevenson (Glasgow) octogenarian elected to the Hall of Fame in 1986, Richard Bacon (Streatham), Bob Kenyon (Blackpool), Barry Gage (Richmond), John and Pauline Rost (Streatham), Dave Richards (Sobell Centre and London All Stars), the Goldstone family (Streatham) and many more.

Set-backs occurred like the final appearance of Wembley Lions on 30 November 1968 with, as 'Red' de Mesquita, referee, radio commentator and Chief of the London Nuts, commented 'no hint in the programme that the sport would not return after the Christmas break.' At least Lions went out with a 3–0 win over Paisley Mohawks, and at least the rink was not pulled down.

That is what had happened to Brighton's famous Sports Stadium which closed on 23 May 1965, the final match being between Tigers and, again, Paisley Mohawks. That is also what happened to the magnificent 5,000-seater stadium at Beresford Terrace, Ayr, which closed in April 1972.

Sussex Senators were to revive Brighton interest to a certain extent between 1970 and 1973 when, with ex-Tigers like O'Brien, Fresher, Cook and Shepherd, they won the Southern League. They practised at the Rank rink which had no barriers and no seats and had to play all their matches away. Even the Rank rink was closed in October 1972. In 1978 a mini-rink measuring 60 × 40 feet was opened in Brighton, and in 1980 Mike Green formed Brighton Royals. They too played all their matches away. Despite this they were to be strong contenders in their division in the 1980s and developed a high scoring forward in Robert Breskal who made the jump to the Premier Division with Dundee Rockets, later moving to Medway Bears.

Fortunately, another rink opened in Ayr but it was not as large as the Beresford Terrace stadium and not ideal for hockey although the officials and players of Ayr Bruins have persevered and kept the flag flying.

There were other blows of a more personal nature. In 1974 one of hockey's all-time greats, Bobby Lee, died in Brighton, aged 62. He had been happily dividing his time between the golf course and the pub he ran since retiring from the game. A smooth-skating centre, he played with Earls Court Rangers, Quebec Aces, briefly with Montreal Canadiens and then with Brighton Tigers. In the 1946–47 season he set records of 111 points and 54 assists and he also held the English National League records for most points (908) and most assists (436).

After Paisley Mohawks dropped out of competition in 1977–78, Billingham Bombers (later Cleveland Bombers) replaced them. This is a face-off at Billingham.

In 1979 Scottish hockey suffered a great loss with the deaths of three Scots and one Canadian, two of them in car accidents. Bert Nichol, former international and a favourite with Fife Flyers' supporters, was one of those who died.

On a happier note, John Haney was named best goalie although Britain finished last in their Pool in the 1977 World Championships in Copenhagen. Haney was an unexpected bonus, a British passport-holder playing in the Danish League when he offered his services. Later he was to be a co-inventor of the world famous game, Trivial Pursuit.

There were other jewels in the somewhat tarnished crown. Like Jim Franceschini, Italian-Canadian from Mississauga, Ontario, who, after playing with Milan and Herano, joined Altrincham in 1970–71 and stayed with the Aces until 1977, apart from a brief fling with Sheffield Lancers. This smart centreman was second in the scoring race when Aces won the championship in 1973 and again when they were runners-up the following year. In his third campaign he topped 100 points. Jim was last heard of teaching in Brisbane, Australia, but for seven years he left his mark on British hockey.

His final season saw what was probably the best team of the twilight years, the 1976–77 Fife Flyers. They won the 'Icy' Smith Cup by defeating Southampton Vikings and, as winners of the Northern League, Northern Autumn and Spring Cups,

Two of the Lovell hockey dynasty founded by pre-war Scottish League star, Les Lovell: Lawrie (top) and Lindsay (bottom).

became the first team to accomplish a clean sweep since Murrayfield in 1970–71 and only the third in history, Paisley having done it in 1967–68. (Paisley who, for five years, had been playing home matches at Crossmyloof, dropped out of competition in 1977–78, being replaced by Billingham Bombers.)

The all-conquering Fife team deserves to be remembered by posterity: John Pullar, Willie Cottrell; Joe McIntosh, Brian Peat, Dave Medd, Angus Cargill, Ally Brennan; Lawrie Lovell (coach), Dougie Latto, Jimmy Jack, Les Lovell (captain), Chic Cottrell, Ken Horne, Gordon Latto, Jack Latto (manager). Four of this team would still be with Flyers when they reached the Bluecol Cup Final in 1984 – Gordon and Dougie Latto, Chic Cottrell and Brian Peat.

With all the difficulties they faced, London Phoenix Flyers had to be quite a team to win the Inter-City League from Southampton Vikings and Streatham Redskins in 1979–80. They had to play most of their home games (at Richmond) at 11 p.m. which meant that rarely more than 150 spectators turned up. The one match they played at a more reasonable hour attracted nearly 1,000 spectators. Vikings, on the other hand, played to around 10,000 spectators in twelve home games. A French-Canadian, Bob Bechard, was Flyers' top scorer, and their other leading marksmen, Billy Walker and Dave Howden, were also Canadians. Goalminder Charlie Colon and All Star defenceman Chris Scammon were American, so Flyers had a lot of overseas players compared with Fife's native sons. Colon, a very good goalie, is still playing in the British League today.

By 1979 things were happening in Dundee a man with claim to being the sport's top enthusiast, Tom Stewart, was sponsoring international tournaments including the GB Open Challenge Cup and the Four Nations Cup.

When the Canadian Concordia Stingers won the GB Open Challenge by beating Holland, Denmark and Great Britain, there was a bonus for Tom and his Dundee Rockets because three of the Stingers would sign for Dundee in due course – Roy Halpin, Chris Brinster and Kevin O'Neill. Halpin was to become one of the great stars of modern British hockey. (The trophy, incidentally, was presented by Marsh Key, Dundee and Harringay centreman of the 1950s.)

An Old Timers Tournament was held at Kirkcaldy in March 1980, twenty-four teams from Canada, USA, Sweden, Finland, Holland and Great Britain taking part, the Finns being overall winners.

In a game which brought back memories to many followers of the sport, Scotland's 'Grouse-beaters' lost in overtime to Central Ontario Over-Fifties. The home team included Bill Sneddon, Billy Brennan, Lawrie and Les Lovell, Tom Stewart, Jackie Dryburgh and Harold 'Pep' Young. Central Ontario had Randy Ellis (Dunfermline), Bobby Burns (Dundee and Edinburgh), Gord Blackman (Falkirk and Edinburgh), Ed Mitchell (Dunfermline and Dundee), Len Gaudette (Brighton and Dunfermline) and Max Richardson (Fife).

There were also six England v. Scotland matches that season, and Scotland won five of them.

Another group of old-timers, English this time, went to the Middle East to demonstrate ice hockey to the Arabs. A British firm had built the first ice rink in the desert, in Baghdad. Years afterwards, British puck-chasers 'opened' a rink in Kuwait, oil-rich country on the Persian Gulf. The party included Mike O'Brien, Rupe Fresher, Harry Pearson, John Cook, Tony Whitehead, Fred Sandford, Tony Goldstone, Dave and Gerry Richards, Jeff Smith and John Rego, managed by Clive 'Nipper' Millard. They played two fifteen-minute exhibition games each night with the older players representing Kuwait and the younger ones England. Diplomatically, the boys made sure 'Kuwait' won most of the time.

Names in the news as the 1980s dawned with the future looking bright were Robin Andrew, a great defenceman with Aviemore; a Canadian, Glen Skidmore, going well with Solihull; and a player-coach Alex Dampier, on the ball (or rather the puck) with Murrayfield. Englishman Gary Keward, who had spent some time in Canada and was now managing Sheffield Lancers, was locked in negotiations to bring the sport back to Nottingham. When he succeeded, most of the Sheffield team would go with him including his son Dwayne, Lancers' leading scorer. Southampton's 33-year-old Colin Bennett clocked up ten seasons and scored 136 goals in 102 games.

Odd spot When Murrayfield Racers met Billingham Bombers in the Northern Autumn Cup play-offs, a shot from Alex Dampier hit Bombers' reserve goalie, Paul Barker, so hard that it ricocheted off the netman into the crowd and struck a woman spectator on the shoulder. Both required hospital treatment, Barker receiving eight stitches.

12 THE BIG LEAGUE

It was a dark, wet and miserable night in London in October 1982. The rain was bucketing down, the streets were awash with water and most citizens of good sense were safely tucked up at home with a book, a blonde or a bucket of cocoa, according to taste. But as I left Streatham Ice Rink on the long drive back to Norfolk there was a song in my heart. It was not entirely due to the warm hospitality which the Streatham Ice Hockey Club was lavishing on its guests, mostly from the Press, as an introduction to the new season. Rather was it because almost everyone I met that evening, old friends and new, and everything that was discussed that evening, served to convince me that ice hockey really was back on the road to success.

The new BIHA President Fred Meredith had been there, accompanied by BIHA Secretary Pat Marsh, a young lady whose loyalty to the sport over the years is almost beyond belief. When Fred stood up to speak it was to announce that there were now 30 clubs affiliated to the BIHA, mustering between them 80 teams and more than 2,000 players. The Juniors had performed creditably in the World Championships and had won the Fair Play Cup. The BIHA had signed a big television deal with Thames TV and ITV Sport: there was to be a special TV Cup competition, a televised England v. Scotland international, and some televised League action. All this, plus the Lee Valley rink opening in North-East London in August 1983.

That was the good news in 1982 and in the succeeding years it was to get better all the time.

Posterity may have a good word or two to say about this fellow Meredith. In a Richmond press release for Oxford University v. Cambridge 17 February 1958, No. 1 for Cambridge is described thus: *Fred Meredith*. Trinity College, where he is studying economics and law. A Canadian (born Montreal, 1937) he was formerly at Bishop's College School, PQ, and played intermediate and high school senior hockey. First year with team. *Goat* or defence.

If you subscribe to the theory that all goalminders are crazy, then 'goat' he was; he played three years in the nets for Cambridge (which shows he was brave) and then took over as coach, the Light Blues having the longest run of success in their history. Cambridge won four out of five Varsity duels under Fred, and when he decided to settle down in Britain he worked valiantly on behalf of the BIHA during the twilight years even being Secretary for a time. When he succeeded 'Bunny' Ahearne as President he went to work on securing major sponsorship for the sport using all his knowledge gained as a management consultant. Just how well he did is now a matter of record.

The come-back story really began with the dawn of the 1980s. The 1981–82 season saw both the English and the Scottish National Leagues revived, twenty-one years after the original British League expired, more than twenty-five since the old English and Scottish League competitions had been held.

The top four teams, Streatham Redskins and Blackpool Seagulls from England, Murrayfield Racers and Dundee Rockets from Scotland, met at Streatham to contest the right to be called British Champions.

The rink, resplendent in its new furnishings and décor, provided an excellent setting; there was television coverage, and the Championships had a sponsor, Wilson's Top Brass Lager, who ensured that everything was done to make it an occasion to remember. The semi-finals went to form. Dundee, the Scottish champions, comfortably defeated Blackpool 16–4, but Streatham had a tougher time overcoming Murrayfield 9–5, a crucial moment coming when Streatham goalie, Gary Brine, saved a penalty-shot.

A full house saw a titanic struggle between Redskins and Rockets in the final. Streatham led 2–1 midway through the last period, but Rockets fought back to score two goals in sixteen seconds. The Dundee roll of honour: Mike Ward, Bill Stewart (goal); Doug Scrimgeour, Bill Murray, Jock McGuff, Chris Brinster, Graeme Lafferty, Kevin O'Neill, George Reid (captain), Roy Halpin, Charlie Kinmond, Steve Garigan, Joe Guilcher, Scott Hudson, Sandy Bruce, Graeme Stewart, Ronnie Wood, Ally Wood, Fraser Wilson; Tom Stewart (manager), J. Lumsden (trainer), J. Hudson (assistant trainer).

Glynne Thomas, on the roster as one of Streatham's goalies, decided to hang up his pads when the new season dawned. He was 47 and had had a remarkable career starting with Richmond Juniors in 1949, moving up to the Ambassadors the following year and playing for England Under-17. In 1955 he moved to Liverpool Leopards and six years later played for Great Britain in the World Championships. He was with Southampton Vikings in 1962, moved to Wembley Lions in 1963 and was named Player of the Year. He then retired but could not stay away from the game joining Streatham in 1972 and staying there until his final retirement. He was chosen again for Great Britain in 1976. Glynne's pads and other gear went to help a British youngster take up the game.

Old stars bowed out, new ones came in. Streatham had a 23-year-old goalscorer from Canada named Gary Stefan; Nottingham had a top goalie who had emigrated from the North-East in Frankie Killen; and so it went on round the circuit. The news on the rink front was equally encouraging. The East of England rink at Peterborough had got off to a great start, and plans were in hand for the first Welsh rink at Cardiff.

It was in this buoyant atmosphere that the decision was taken to revive the British League, but bearing in mind the lessons of the past it was decided to split the League into sections in order to minimise travelling time and costs.

Fifteen clubs formed the First Division. In Section A were the main Scots teams – Ayr, Dundee, Fife, Glasgow and Murrayfield. Section B had Cleveland, Durham, Whitley, Nottingham and Streatham; C included Altrincham, Blackpool, Crowtree, Richmond and Southampton.

The Second Division had Northern and Southern Sections, Bradford, Deeside, Grimsby and Sheffield being in the former, Bristol, Peterborough, Solihull and Streatham Bruins in the latter.

Streatham Braves (Under-13) rest from their exertions in the dressing-room.

There was also a Third Division comprising mainly reserve teams plus the two universities. Brighton were back in this division but as the Royals ('we couldn't call them Tigers, that would be sacrilege' said player-coach Mike Green).

A step to advance the long-term future of the game came with the revival after thirty-one years of an English Junior League, again in two Sections – Bradford, Sunderland Arrows, Grimsby Dynamos (champions of the junior Inter-City League the previous season) and Nottingham Cougars, newcomers coached by Les Strongman, Harry Todd and Steve Matthews, in the North; Brighton Tiger-Cubs, Peterborough Jets, Richmond Falcons, Streatham Scorpions and Southampton Junior Vikings in the South.

A bonus was the return of Bournemouth Stags under the guidance of veteran of the hockey wars, Colin Bennett, and recruited largely from former Southampton and Bristol players.

When the smoke cleared at the end of a very full season, Dundee Rockets were the winners of Section A, Durham Wasps

Goalmouth action in a 1986 match between two teams whose histories go back to the 1930s – Southampton and Richmond

top of Section B and Altrincham Aces leaders of Section C. In the play-offs for the British Championships, held at Streatham, Dundee emerged as winners with Durham runners-up.

Although Dundee again emphasised how important team-work was to them, it has to be said that their chief inspiration was Roy Halpin. 'Roy of the Rockets', not very big at 5 feet 8 inches and 163lb, knew what he was doing around the net. On April 4 1982 he scored 14 goals against Durham Wasps and set a League record of 151 goals and 254 points in 48 games. He was top scorer again the following season with 162 points and in the next campaign boosted his figure to 234 points.

Halpin caught the eye of Toronto Maple Leafs at one time but put his studies ahead of hockey. He first came to Britain with Concordia University Stingers, played a season in Japan ('Respect for age is such that a younger player is morally bound to pass the puck to an older one') and joined Dundee because he liked the golf. Forced to retire through injury, he was voted into Britain's Hall of Fame and is now a sports organiser in Canada.

Dundee became the first British team to participate in the European Cup, open to the champions of each country, but the gap between Britain and most of the Continental teams was still a wide one and it is best to cast a veil over the proceedings.

Grimsby won the Junior Championships, beating Streatham in the play-offs, although the South Londoners won the Pee-Wee title.

Justification of the junior policy was that a number of the players involved subsequently made the senior grade, among them Grimsby goaltender John Wolfe (16), Brighton's Bob Breskal (16) and Streatham players, Andy Leggatt (15) and Brian Biddulph (16). Defenceman Biddulph represented Great Britain in the European Junior Championships, the first coloured player to do so.

· Evidence of the enthusiasm that still existed for the sport in Brighton and other areas was given by a rink hockey match at the Brighton Conference Centre in which Brighton BHV Bengals defeated Crystal Palace 5−1. Nearly 2,000 people turned out, most of them former ice hockey enthusiasts. Players from the great days of Brighton Tigers were introduced – Gib Hutchinson, Lennie Baker, 'Lefty' Wilmot, Freddie Sutherland, Jack McDonald. Slightly younger ones played an exhibition game – Ray Partridge, Roger Turner, Roy Shepherd, Roy Yates, Roy Harnett, John Rost, John Baxter, John Cook, Jackie Dryburgh, Harry Pearson, 'Red' Imrie.

I was invited to tend goal during this match but chickened out at the last moment, much to the disappointment of referee

Norman de Mesquita who had been looking forward to sending me to the sin-bin. Norman took his revenge on my one-time assistant, Mike Dunton, playing for Crystal Palace, who was sent off for 'roughing'.

Apart from Halpin, players who hit the headlines during the season included Roy's team-mate, Al Leblanc, Jim Earle, and Ted Phillips, from Cleveland, Gary Stefan and English team-mate Tony Goldstone from Streatham, Neil McKay, Nottingham, Ronnie Wood, Dundee, and the Sims twins, Bruce and Brian, from Blackpool. Goaltenders who did well included Katerynuk, Durham, Keward, Nottingham, and Terry Ward, Cleveland.

The Championship play-offs were sponsored this time by Heineken, and with the new season came the exciting news that the same company would sponsor the British League, which would in future be known as the Heineken League. The sponsors did the job properly. Money was pumped into the sport, much of it to develop young home-grown talent. Special awards were introduced, a regular press service set up, clubs given aid with programmes and with travel expenses. It opened up a whole new future for the game.

Other big sponsors came in. The Autumn Cup was sponsored by Bluecol for a season and then the Norwich Union took over. Imperial Tobacco backed the Regal Scottish Cup, Fosters Menswear sponsored the Midlands League and Whitbread Best Scotch supported the Castle Eden Cup for the North-East clubs. Nearly every League club had individual sponsors, some of them very big companies indeed. Ice hockey had moved into the big league.

Sponsors don't throw their money away, they expect a good return – so why ice hockey? Andrew Harrowven, Sponsorships Co-ordinator of the giant Norwich Union Insurance Group, told me: 'When Norwich Union was asked to sponsor what was then called the Autumn Cup, we had to think long and hard as to whether it was the right sport for us. Later, having decided that ice hockey would help us project the image we wanted, we still approached that first Norwich Union Cup fixture in September 1985 with considerable nervousness.

'The setting was all so new and we couldn't be sure of the welcome we would get at the rinks or, indeed, what kind of response to expect from the clubs themselves. Then there was the worry about the standard of hospitality for our guests and even whether they would actually enjoy watching ice hockey.

'We needn't have worried. A warm reception was given to us everywhere we went and the game itself certainly won more

Ron Plumb (3), player-coach of Fife Flyers, and Bruce McDonagh (6), Cleveland Bombers, in action during the 1984–85 season. Plumb, a skilled rearguard, played professional hockey in the NHL and in the now-defunct World Hockey Association.

fans from our side of the rink. We could not have had a better introduction to the sport with cliff hanging matches and an exciting first Norwich Union Cup Final.

'Such was our media coverage in particular and the increased stature of the game in general as attendances increased by more than twenty per cent, that we felt able to take the second Norwich Union Cup Final to the prestigious stage of the National Exhibition Centre in Birmingham. A costly exercise, almost an experiment, but we were desperately keen for it to succeed. And succeed it did as nearly 6,000 fans watched another memorable final and over four million more joined them from television armchairs to see Nottingham Panthers edging out Fife Flyers in extra time. If our first season in ice hockey had been one of anticipation and pleasure in making so many new and friendly contacts, the second was one of building on those new relationships in a way which surpassed our expectations.

'Now we feel that the name Norwich Union has become

synonymous with excitement and fair play in sport and we aim
to keep it that way.

'It's getting on for two hundred years since an enterprising
business man sowed the seeds of today's huge Norwich Union
Insurance Group which continues to go from strength to
strength. From the rink-sides we can't look forward two centuries, but we are sure that the enterprise of Norwich Union's
partnership with ice hockey will progress as season succeeds
season.'

In this atmosphere the game has flourished. Dundee Rockets
were British Champions again in 1983–84 having headed the
League regular schedule, with Murrayfield Racers as runners-up.
The following season, although Durham Wasps were top in the
regular schedule, Fife Flyers won the play-offs, with Murrayfield again runners-up. Murrayfield finally became brides
instead of bridesmaids in 1985–86 when, although Durham
again headed the regular schedule, Racers became Champions
by beating Dundee 4–2 in the final of six-team play-offs.

During the same seasons, Durham won the Bluecol Autumn
Cup, lost to Racers (at Murrayfield) for the same competition,
now renamed the Norwich Union Cup, and saw Nottingham
Panthers take the trophy in the first final at the Birmingham
National Exhibition Centre. The Cup switch to the NEC and
the move of the British Championship to Wembley was no
reflection on Streatham and its owners, Mecca Leisure. The
South London rink is smart and well-furbished and the ice pad
one of the best and largest, but, alas, spectator accommodation
is limited and insufficient to cater for the thousands who want
to see the play-offs.

When the 1986–87 season dawned, the British Ice Hockey
Association was able to announce that more teams would be
taking part in the British League than ever before in the history
of the sport.

The Premier Division comprised Murrayfield Racers, Dundee
Rockets, Fife Flyers, Ayr Bruins, Durham Wasps, Whitley War-
riors, Cleveland Bombers, Nottingham Panthers, Solihull
Barons and Streatham Redskins, ten teams in all.

The First Division had no less than sixteen teams: Kirkcaldy
Kestrels, Glasgow Eagles, Irvine Wings, Sunderland Chiefs,
Blackpool Seagulls, Altrincham Aces, Peterborough Pirates, Tel-
ford Tigers, Oxford Stars, Swindon Wildcats, Slough Jets, Lee
Valley Lions, Richmond Flyers, Medway Bears, Southampton
Vikings and Bournemouth Stags.

Division Two, divided into North, South and Midland Sections, had twenty-three teams, bringing the total in the League

to an all-time high of forty-nine. Division Two North had Billingham Buccaneers, Bradford Bulldogs, Durham Hornets, Grimsby Buffaloes, Nottingham Trojans, Sunderland Tomahawks and Whitley Bay Bandits. Midlands comprised Ashfield Islanders, Bristol Phantoms, Cardiff Devils, Deeside Dragons, Peterborough Titans, Solihull Knights, Telford Tornadoes and Trafford Tigers. South had Bournemouth Bucks, Brighton Royals, Hastings Arrows, Medway Marauders, Oxford City Satellites, Richmond Raiders, Southampton Vikings 2 and Streatham Bruins.

In addition to the forty-nine League clubs there were also teams at Oxford and Cambridge Universities, Aviemore and elsewhere.

Moreover, the BIHA were able to announce with confidence that an extra Division would be created in 1987–88 since five new rinks – Basingstoke, Chelmsford, Romford, Livingston and Belfast – would be opening within twelve months. The new season had hardly started when a new 3,000 seater rink was announced to be located between Ayr and Prestwick and destined as the home of Ayr Bruins.

Parallel with this growth was the great development in junior and pee-wee hockey, culminating in 1986 with the first British Junior League Championship play-offs at Wembley between the English Champions, Streatham Scorpions, and the Scottish Champions, Fife Flames. Streatham, who included Warren Rost, grandson of the legendary 'Sonny' Rost, won 7–0. The English Pee-Wee play-offs were won by Durham Midges who defeated Bournemouth Terriers 5–1.

Charles Gimmer, Ice Hockey World reporter, Lee Valley announcer and programme compiler, and former player with Harringay Hornets, Streatham and Earls Court Marlboroughs, whose grandson Jon Beckett plays for Streatham, sees a great contrast between the opportunities now given to youngsters to learn the game and the limited chances of yester-year:

'Nowadays, youngsters generally start their hockey careers soon after six years of age. They are pampered by their parents and the best possible equipment available is lavished upon them. Regular coaching sessions are made available, plus the opportunity of attendance at hockey schools. A pee-wee set-up for under-13s and a junior one for them to move to at 13 until 16 is the usual progression, and after this they could be selected to play in their club's top team, often a Premier Division outfit. If not quite good enough they often get the chance to play in the reserve team in the Second Division or move to another club's First Division team.

'This was not the case fifty years ago. In the 1930s hockey was just making its first real impact with the coming to London of Wembley, Earls Court's Empress Hall and the super Harringay Arena. The promoters of these establishments did encourage boys' hockey, but in those days times were hard. Many parents just weren't interested and certainly couldn't afford to finance their son's hockey ambitions. If a youngster wanted to play badly enough he had to do it himself, so most lads didn't start to play until they left school at the age of 14. He had to find a job which provided sufficient money to buy skates, the first requirement. The cheapest of these were priced at twenty-two shillings and sixpence, a week's wages for some people. Sticks were cajoled from top-class players, and discarded ones repaired as best possible. The rest of the kit was mostly home-made, using football shinguards and the like.

'The usual thing was to form the kids at any one rink into say four teams in a house league. When other rinks challenged, the pick of the four teams made one representative side. Older players over the age of 16 performed in the National Provincial League which provided a standard of hockey approximating to modern Second Division quality.

'Amongst the better players developed by this system were, notably, Arthur Green, who was a Wembley product and who captained Wembley Lions later in post-war years, his stablemate John Oxley, now deceased, also played for Lions and later Brighton Tigers. Both were well up to the standard of Canadians who formed the bulk of all teams until the big shutdown in the late 1950s.

'In Scotland, though, the local lads were very well looked after if those who emanated from junior ranks are anything to judge by; such names as Tuck and Tiny Syme, 'Red' Imrie, Jack Dryburgh, Marshall Key, Johnny Carlyle and a host of others who subsequently figured prominently in post-war days. These Scottish lads performed most efficiently in our leading clubs both north and south of the border.

'Looking back on the year of 1939 and earlier days brings back happy memories, no parental power with pressure to succeed at all costs, no suspicion of favouritism by managers, just try and learn from your coach and go out and enjoy your hockey and keep it clean, win or lose.

'Today, kids' hockey is tougher. Managers of pee-wee and junior teams will tell you that they don't play recreational hockey, but are geared up to produce quality players of Premier Division standard.'

From the long-term viewpoint of British hockey who can

Tony Hand, Murrayfield Racers: the first British born-and-bred Heineken League player to be a draft choice for an NHL professional club.

deny that today's managers and coaches are right? The system is now producing lots of reasonable players against a comparative handful thirty or forty years ago. But there is a long way to go. The Syme brothers, Arthur Green, Johnnie Oxley, 'Fish' Robertson and others of their generation were good enough to play in what was a very high-quality British game. There is still only a handful good enough to play in the best circles outside Britain. At the present rate of progress, however, the day will come when British players can hold their own with the best of other countries.

The shining example for all British born-and-bred players to emulate is Tony Hand, youthful star of Murrayfield Racers and first man to tot up more than 400 points in the Heineken Premier League. In 1986 he became the first British Heineken League player to be drafted by an NHL professional club when the champion Edmonton Oilers made him their final choice. Although Hand was one of those axed when Edmonton's training camp closed, the fact that the Oilers chose him at all says a lot for the young man's ability and must be a great encouragement to others.

Tony's elder brother Paul also plays with Racers and his younger one David shows promise. All three owe much to their widowed mother, Lorraine, an Edinburgh nurse, who has worked hard to give all three boys their chance in hockey.

However, the yardstick for progress of English and Scottish players (and hopefully in the future, now they have ice, Welsh and Irish too) is no longer necessarily Canada. Most European countries made tremendous progress during the years the game was virtually at a standstill in Great Britain as successive British champions have found to their cost.

The European Cup is open to the winner of each European league, but it was not until 1983 that Britain first took up her option with Dundee Rockets carrying the flag. However, the Rockets were outclassed in the first round both then and again the following season, despite including Paul and Tony Hand on the second occasion. Third time out, Durham Wasps did rather better, beating the Yugoslav champions, HC Jesenice, 7–6 at home and losing 8–3 away, to go down 14–10 on aggregate. Wasps could not keep it up in the 1986–87 season, however, going down to the Norwegian champions, Stjernen Oslo, 23–7 on aggregate. So there is obviously a long way to go.

On the other side of the coin, Great Britain won Pool C of the European Junior Championships (under 19) in 1986, beating Spain 6–3 and 5–3, losing 4–3 to Hungary and defeating the same country 3–1, thus earning promotion to Pool B for the

Stephen Cooper, Durham Wasps, voted best defenceman in Pool C of the World Junior Championships 1986, picks up the puck behind his own net as goalie Frankie Killen looks on.

1987 Championships, Holland being relegated to Pool C. The overall champions, incidentally, were Finland, followed by Sweden, Czechoslovakia and USSR, an indication of how young hockey power is developing.

The British team, the oldest of whom was 17, was as follows (mark the names well, they should be the stars of the Heineken League during the next decade or so): Martin McKay (Dundee), Barry Spours (Streatham) in goal; Blair Kelly, Richard Phillips (Kirkcaldy), Jim Johnston, Warren Rost (Streatham), Robert Wilkinson (Durham), Ian Boyer (captain) (Solihull), Jason Martin (Nottingham), Colin McHaffie (Ayr), Frazer Hopper (Streatham), Ian Cooper, Anthony Johnson (Durham), Sean Doherty, Lee Elliott (Sunderland), Grant Mitchell (Sheffield), Grant Slater (Dundee), Kevin King (Glasgow), Dean Edmiston, Bobby Haig (Kirkcaldy). Lawrie Lovell was coach, John Rost and Brian Cooper, managers.

In the World Junior (under-20) Championships, also competing in Pool C, Britain won the bronze medal, finishing third to France and Denmark and ahead of China, Hungary and Belgium. Alex Dampier coached the team and on this occasion had two assistants, Pete Johnson (Durham) and Terry Matthews (Whitley). Dundee's McKay did most of the goal-tending, with Ian Young playing 90 minutes and Spours just the standby on this occasion. Tony Hand scored ten of Britain's twenty goals and finished fourth overall in the scoring table, while Stephen Cooper was rated the best defenceman in the Pool and voted to the All Star team.

The decisive match was the 14−2 hammering at the hands of France, ten of the goals coming whilst the British team was short-handed. 'The ref didn't understand our style', said Dampier.

Britain were outshot in most of their five games, but McKay and Young played splendidly, justifying their senior outings. McKay hit the headlines again on 28 December 1986 when, after starting the game against Ayr Bruins in the nets, he later changed into 'out-players' kit and scored a goal in the final minutes of the game which Rockets won 12−1. The BIHA decided that this was illegal under the rule which says that a list of players and goalkeepers shall be handed to the referee before the game and no change shall be permitted after the commencement of the game. The result was allowed to stand, but the Dundee coach was reprimanded.

Apart from McKay, Cooper and, of course, Hand, I must admit to being impressed with Edmiston and Haig, of Kirkcaldy, who show every sign of becoming established in senior hockey.

In the 1980s women's hockey came into its own with the formation of an English Womens' League. It owed much to the efforts of a handful of girls led by Sue Parsons, of Streatham. Her team, Streatham Strikers, 1985−86 champions; Peterborough Ravens, 1984−85 champions; and Solihull Vixens, have been the pick of the crop thus far. Oxford and Cambridge Universities, Brighton Amazons and Oxford City Rockets are also in the League, and Telford Tigresses and Deeside are expected to swell the ranks.

Womens' hockey goes back a long way, almost as far as the game itself. In 1899 a hockey writer reported that there were so many ladies' teams in Canada that 'only the slowest, smallest towns did not glory in such clubs'.

A.C.A. Wade, pioneer hockey and skating reporter, recalls a match at Grosvenor House in the 1930s between France and England and an English reporter asking the French girls who had just scored for them. The reply came, 'C'est cinq, Monsieur,' obviously referring to the player numbers in the programme. 'What did she say — they've sank?' muttered the bewildered reporter, doubtless a graduate of a school of journalism.

Charlie Sumner's wife, Grace, who played in later years for Harringay Huskies and Streatham Felines, recalls: 'Pre-war

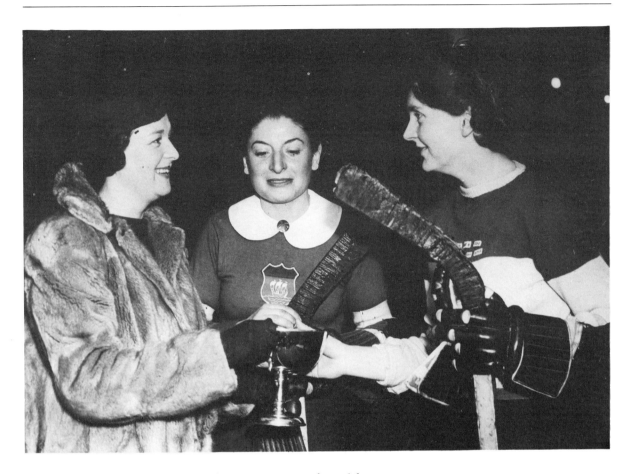

ladies' hockey was in the main the prerogative of wealthy young socialites, and there was, in effect, only one team which moved from rink to rink before finding a permanent home at Harringay Arena where a few, a very few, local girls were invited to join. They were coached at various times by 'Fan' Heximer, Jimmy Foster and Dunc Cheyne.

'Most of them had picked up the game in Switzerland or at finishing schools and universities on the Continent. Mona Friedlander, at centre, was a qualified pilot who owned her own plane. Muriel Low, left-wing, played cricket for England and rode her motor cycle from the Midlands to Harringay. Jean Bayes, the captain, was a teacher at the School of Heraldry and daughter of the famous sculptor, Gilbert Bayes.

'There was keen rivalry from the French who were fairly evenly matched. When the teams met for the last time in 1939 for the Lady Greer Silver Rose Bowl, England won 3−0 to retain the trophy outright.

Lady Greer presenting the Greer Trophy to Jean Bayes, captain of the England womens' team, after they had won it outright in 1939. French captain Collette Raymondeau is in the middle.

A man in a dirty raincoat lurks in the background as the girls prepare for the first post-war women's match between Streatham Felines and Harringay Huskies in 1949. However, he's no intruder but their coach, Charlie Sumner.

Peterborough Ravens, one of the best modern women's hockey teams. The team shown were joint League Champions in 1983–84.

'After the war, the Streatham and Harringay clubs were formed with a few of the pre-war players but mostly local girls. At Harringay there were novelty matches against Racers and Greyhounds, with the men playing with brooms instead of hockey sticks. Unfortunately there was so much demand on ice time to train boy players that by 1953 the girls were ousted, not to appear again until the 1980s.'

Grace thinks that you would not know that they are girls playing today, hidden by their helmets and other gear. 'In the old days girls would take the ice with their hair set in the latest fashion and full make-up, adding a glamorous touch to the game. Their skill on skates and stick-handling was, in comparison to the current crop of girl players, superior in all respects.' That sounds like fighting-talk, ladies!

A lady goalie made hockey history in the 1985–86 season. On Sunday 29 December Oxford City Stars were due to play at home in a Fosters Midlands League match, their opponents being Solihull Barons. Due to an administrative mix-up by the then Oxford management, most of the Stars failed to appear and Oxford were forced to ice a team comprising one of their first team goalies, Mike Kellond, and regular forward Jamie Cameron, the remainder being juniors apart from Paul Dudley and Paul Spencer.

Solihull were in a dilemma since the sponsors, Fosters Menswear, had a number of guests present. So, correctly in most people's view, the Barons went all out for goals and, in due course, they hit the fifty target.

After two periods of incessant battering, Kellond was exhausted – and into the breach stepped Emma Bowles, who had already played one match earlier in the evening, for Oxford Rockets against Solihull Vixens. She thus became the first girl to play in a competitive men's match in Great Britain, and – perhaps – in the world.

In 1972 Canadian writer Andy O'Brien dedicated his book on Canadiens' netman Jacques Plante to 'Sandra, a very young lady of Dearborn, Michigan . . . the only girl goalie I know in the whole of hockeydom.' Either Mr O'Brien has led a sheltered life or else he meant the only girl goalie on a men's team. In which case our Emma is second.

Oxford lost by a record score, 50–0, but Kellond and Emma were voted Oxford's Players of the Match – quite right too! The Solihull tally beat the previous British record score set two months previously when Medway Bears defeated Richmond Flyers 48–2.

In October 1986 the Missisagua Senior Recreational team played five 'non-contact' games in Britain, the first Canadian women's team to play in this country. They were led by their founder, Mabel Boyd, still playing at the age of 65.

Dave Stoyanovich, Fife Flyers, a devastating winger with one of the hardest shots in the League. Here he scores against Cleveland Bombers.

Jeff Smith, Streatham netminder, kicks away a shot from Murrayfield danger-man Rick Fera while Darren Zinger gives cover.

At the other end of the hockey scale the Heineken League is gradually attracting good-class hockey players not only from Canada but from Finland, Germany, Czechoslovakia and other European countries. While imports are limited to three per team this can be no bad thing, giving British youngsters a chance to learn from the best. The danger will come if unrestricted

Dean Vogelgesang and fellow Solihull
Barons celebrate a goal against
Peterborough Pirates.

Murrayfield v. Streatham. Hanson
saves from Richard Bacon, veteran
Redskin forward, later their coach.

1986 DASCO British Rookie of the Year, Nigel Rhodes (Nottingham Panthers) fires one at Craig Dickson in the Fife nets.

imports are allowed and the home-bred player gets frozen out, as was often the case prior to the Second World War.

In recent seasons Gary Unger, durable 'Iron Man' of the top professional National Hockey League, has played with Dundee and Peterborough; another professional veteran Ron Plumb has been a double success on defence and coaching Fife; and Flyers have also had a winger on Montreal's list, Dave Stoyanovich, a devastating winger with one of the hardest shots in the game. Fred Perlini, with the 1986–87 Nottingham Panthers, had a brief whirl with Toronto Maple Leafs and three seasons in the next best professional set-up, the American Hockey League. At the same time, Dundee iced Czech veteran, Jaroslav Lycka, a heady player who, by his ability to pace a game and slow up the action when necessary, brought back memories of past greats like Len Burrage.

Referees, in particular Terry Gregson, have been brought over from the professional ranks to coach British officials, and Dundee's Tom Stewart arranged for New York Ranger star Rod

Gilbert to come over and conduct a junior coaching clinic.

How would the moderns fare against the stars of the Golden Age before the Second World War? Not very well, thinks BIHA Vice-President Ernie Ramus, who as a left-winger played on the Streatham team which won the National League in 1934–35 and were European Club Champions and winners of the Berlin Invitation Tournament. Ernie also played on the Great Britain team which won the World bronze and European silver in 1935 and also turned out for Queens and Princes during an illustrious career. He thinks today's game is faster as a spectacle but the stick-handling is less precise, the passing and shooting less accurate and the marking not so close. He disapproves of the slap shot, the red line, the modern stick and the loose interpretation of the rules, particularly as they relate to interference and boarding. Is Ramus, born in Ottawa but a long-time resident in England, right?

What would be the result if the best of one era were pitted against the best of another? Most sports authors cannot resist the temptation to pick 'the greatest of all time' and I'm just as weak as the next guy. So I have picked three teams, one from the 1930s, another from the 1940s and 1950s and one from the 1980s. I'm not old enough to have seen top-class hockey prior to 1936, whilst the period between the collapse of the old British League and the revival of the new was indeed a twilight age. So here are my teams:

George Reid, veteran Dundee captain, holds the Heineken British Ice Hockey Championship trophy high in triumph.

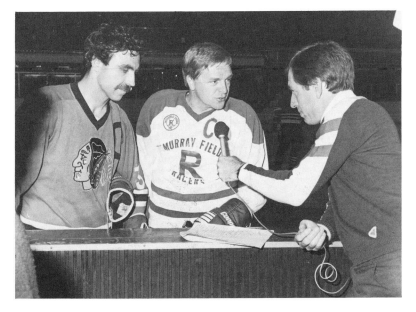

Derek Thomson, of Thames Television, interviews Robin Andrew, captain of Streatham, and Derek Reilly, captain of Murrayfield, before the final of the Red Mountain Cup.

Clap hands and all fall down: Craig Melançon and Dave Rapley combined to score for Streatham despite the defensive tactics of Cleveland's Jim Earle (12), Charlie Colon (4), Cal Land (21) and Gordon Sharpe.

The Golden Boys (1930s)

Jimmy Foster (Richmond and Harringay), Johnny Lacelle (Manchester) in goal; Len Burrage (Harringay), Frank Currie (Richmond, Harringay and Earls Court), Dick Adolph (Harringay), Leo Lamoureux (Earls Court) on defence; Joe Beaton (Richmond and Harringay), Bert Peer (Harringay), Joe Shack (Harringay); Don Willson (Earls Court), Bobby Walton (Wembley), Bert Lemay (Wembley), forwards; Connie Tudin (Harringay), utility.

It is with reluctance that I omit goalies such as Andy Goldie and Maurice Gerth, defencemen like 'Lou' Bates, Bob McCranor and 'Dutch' Behling and forwards such as Joe Brown, Wally Monson, Dunc Cheyne and 'Sparky' Nicholson. But what a bench they would make!

The Boom-time Aces (1940s and 1950s)

'Pete' Belanger (Glasgow, Fife and Harringay), Gib Hutchinson (Wembley and Brighton) in goal; Art Hodgins (Paisley and Streatham), Floyd Snider (Fife), Gordie Poirier (Brighton), 'Duke' Campbell (Brighton, Harringay and Earls Court) on defence; Bobby Lee (Brighton), Bill Glennie (Harringay), Gordie Fashaway (Harringay); 'Chick' Zamick (Nottingham), Bud McEachren (Streatham and Harringay), Les Strongman (Nottingham and Wembley), forwards; Fred Dunsmore (Streatham), utility.

Ed Lochhead, the Paisley netman, blockers like Streatham's Vic Fildes, Bill Winemaster and Don Callaghan and forwards such as Tony Licari, Vic Kreklewetz and Gene Miller could all slot into the team without any loss of power.

The Man in the Mask: Jeff Johnson, netminder of Altrincham Aces is quite a good-looking fellow – but you'd never notice it!

'Just another day at the office,' commented Solihull's Mark Budz after this scrap. He and Streatham's Craig Melançon grapple on the ice while Chris Leggatt is out cold in the background.

Whitley goalie Peter Graham lies back as Peterborough's John Lawless scores one of his many goals.

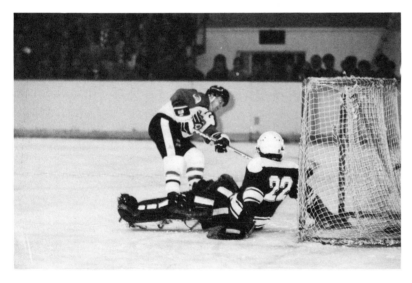

The Moderns (1980s)
Moray Hanson (Murrayfield), Frankie Killen (Nottingham and Durham) in goal; Ron Plumb (Fife), Jaroslav Lycka (Dundee), Chris Kelland (Murrayfield), Stephen Cooper (Durham) on defence; Tony Hand (Murrayfield), Roy Halpin (Dundee), Dave Stoyanovich (Fife); Gary Stefan (Streatham and Slough), Danny Brown (Fife), Jamie Crapper (Durham and Nottingham), forwards; Gary Unger (Dundee and Peterborough), utility.

And we've still left out Colon, Lawless, Earle, Conway, Salmon, Melançon, Slaughter, Bedard and many more.

Who would win? Your guess is as good as mine, probably better.

Meanwhile, what is the view of BIHA President Fred Meredith on the state of the game and its future?

'Ice hockey in Britain is enjoying a period of unprecedented growth – an achievement of which all associated with the sport can feel proud. This progress brings new opportunities, and challenges for success breed ambition – and rightly so. But in looking to the future we must be realistic about our environment and set our goals accordingly.

'As a spectator sport we have outgrown the seating capacity of most rinks. As a participant sport we suffer from a shortage of ice time and facilities, particularly when compared with other countries. Whilst I am certain that Britain can support a network of large multi-purpose arenas in which ice hockey would feature, we have to plan on the basis of what we have.

Lee Valley Lions Geoff Williams (5), Vesa Pennanen (82) and Eddie Joseph (2) guard their goal against Canadian tourists.

'Our overall goals are firstly to improve standards within the sport, playing, coaching, officiating and administration, and secondly to provide an environment in which the sport will grow steadily and in line with its capability to finance that growth.

'What does this mean for the clubs, players and spectators? The structure of the League and other events will continue to evolve but for the top teams it should stabilise within three years. We have the longest season in Europe and that is hard on players and officials. At a minimum, we must organise ourselves to be able to compete effectively at international level and to have two competitive and financially viable top divisions. It is essential that we build on the success of our juniors and compete extensively at international level.

'Expenses continue to rise: club budgets have increased four-fold in as many years. There is a danger that the League could become unbalanced because a few clubs with large seating capacity, major sponsorship or free-spending management seek to spend their way to success. I hope the clubs recognise that the sport cannot afford a situation where it becomes dominated by a few clubs. The BIHA will continue to regulate against it as much as is possible. It will maintain a sponsorship and advertising policy that provides for all clubs to benefit equally from

Nottingham Panthers, surprise winners of the 1986–87 Norwich Union Cup, clear their lines in the first ice hockey match played at the National Exhibition Centre, Birmingham.

Durham's Canadian captain, Mike O'Connor, breaks away from Phil Derbyshire in a 1984 struggle. O'Connor led Wasps to the 1987 Championship.

television coverage, whilst still encouraging individual clubs to seek the rewards of club sponsorship. It will protect the investment of clubs in the training and development of players while at the same time ensuring that new clubs will be able to recruit players with which to establish a viable team. Increasingly it will place emphasis on the concerns of players and officials arising from the developments that are taking place.

'In order to improve playing standards a major effort will be

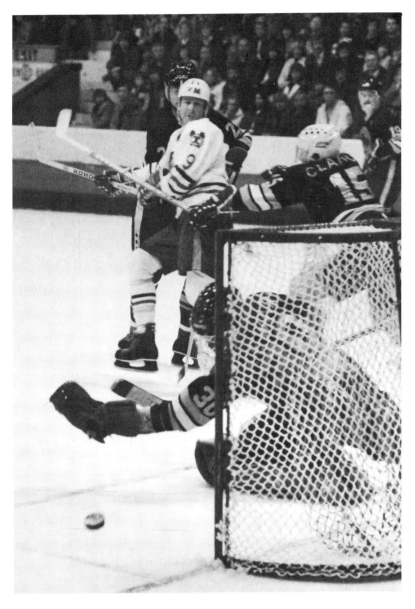

A shot goes wide in a fierce tussle at Nottingham where ice hockey has played to packed houses since Panthers were revived in 1980.

made to train coaches to teach young players the basic skills on which the success of the top ice hockey nations has been founded: training packages will be made available to every club and an education programme introduced. More ice time will be needed and it is hoped that rink management will work with the clubs to increase the number of young players in training, to give them time to practise and play and allow for the introduc-

Dave Stoyanovich, Fife winger, scores against Cleveland Bombers during 1984–85 season. Stoyanovich dressed a few times for the famed Montreal Canadiens in the NHL and came to Scotland from Montreal's farm club.

tion of a third age-bracket for juniors in junior competitions.

'The rapid improvement in playing standards and increase in fixtures has placed a severe strain on officials. They have done well to keep up with the changes that have taken place and will be under pressure for the foreseeable future for they are chasing a fast-moving target. The recruitment, training and development of officials will continue to be given the highest priority. It is an area where clubs will increasingly have to play a bigger part, for example, development of officials must be incorporated within club programmes. I would like to think that the sport could afford a full-time official.

'Ice hockey has made tremendous strides forward in Britain, largely through its own efforts. We have been dependent on a large long-suffering group of enthusiasts; more than ever that support will be needed in the future. However, if we are to make real progress then we will need the full-time professional dedication of experts in areas of major importance – officiating, development, coaching and general administration. The sport is willing to make a major contribution to financing itself, but I believe we have reached the stage where we need and can justify the support of the Sports Council to create a financially stable management structure to take the sport forward. We will be putting over this to them.'

So we come to the end of a collection of memories garnered over years along the Great Ice Way. So many names, so many games, so many stories – enough material for six or seven books.

The time the industrious 'Chick' Hay, of Harringay Racers, came looking for me with blood-lust in his eye because I called him 'ubique' in *Ice Hockey World*. I had to produce a dictionary to prove it wasn't a deadly insult. Then there was Jerrie Cavers, of Greyhounds, pleading with his team-mates to name the miscreant who had the Press calling him 'Gabby'. The boys trying to stifle their laughter because the culprit was sitting next to him on the coach – me! And there was a time when 'Chick' Zamick, Nottingham's all-time great, eyed me askance after the *World* described him as 'a snapper-up of ill-considered trifles'. But Les Anning, then with Wembley Monarchs, rather liked our nickname for him, one which stuck, the 'Rimouski Rocket'.

There were more dangerous moments. In Paris, a Canadian playing with Racing Club, told me just what he was going to do to me, calling me a 'French bastard'. Why he thought London All Stars were stacked with Frenchmen I don't know, but he can't have done much good for Franco-Canadian relations during his stay.

Bobby Lee addressed opponents more politely. At a face-off he would ask, 'How's your mother getting on these days?' While a surprised opponent gathered his thoughts, Bobby whipped the puck away.

The only night I was really apprehensive was not long after the war in a Scottish rink which shall be nameless. In a somewhat violent game, Harringay Racers had beaten the local team and skated off the ice to a storm of boos and howls of rage. I had been handling the team from the bench as 'Duke' Campbell was suffering from flu. With injured defenceman Pat Coburn and out-of-a-team Johnny Beauchamp, both of whom had been sitting with me on the bench, I set off round the rink to the dressing-rooms.

The next moment we were surrounded by an angry mob of women. I never argue with those who say that the female of the species is more deadly than the male – some of these had long hatpins (which I thought had gone out with Queen Victoria) and they were intent on using them. We finally struggled through but all three of us were dishevelled and all three had punctures – in unmentionable parts of our anatomy.

The saddest moment was the time Harringay trainer Harry Aldridge bought a tea-service for his wife when we were touring Czechoslovakia. 'Great country for china' declared Harry. So what happened? On Brno railway station a careless porter dislodged the tea-service from a pile of luggage and we watched horrified as it toppled over the edge of the platform and crashed on to the tracks. I'll never forget the look on poor old Harry's face.

It was all part of life's rich pattern and all part of the greatest game on earth. As Mike Daski, who played with Paisley, Harringay, Ayr, Earls Court, Brighton and Milan back in the 1950s and now coaches in West Germany, wrote to me, 'We sure are fanatics and must love the sport to be part of it so long.'

FURTHER READING

Bass, Howard, *International Encyclopedia of Winter Sports* (Pelham Books, 1971)

Bowman, Bob, *Bob Bowman On The Ice* (Arthur Barker, 1937)

Brodrick, 'Doc', *Ice Hockey* (Nicholas Kaye, 1951)

Drobny, Jaroslav, *Champion In Exile* (SBC, 1957)

Erhardt, Carl, *Ice Hockey* (Foulsham, circa 1938)

Ferguson, Paul, *The Mecca Entertainment Book of Ice Hockey* (David & Charles, 1985)

Fisher, Thomas Knight, *Ice Hockey* (Charles Scribner, 1926)

Fitkin, Ed, *Turk Broda of the Leafs* (Castle, 1950)

Fitkin, Ed, *Max Bentley* (Castle, 1951)

Fitkin, Ed, *Maurice Richard* (Castle, circa 1951)

Fitkin, Ed, *The Gashouse Gang of Hockey* (Castle, circa 1953)

Giddens, Robert, *Ice Hockey, The International Game* (Foyles, 1950)

Hastings, H.C., *Wembley* (Pitkin Pictorials, 1956)

Hewitt, Foster, *Down The Ice* (Philip Allan, 1935)

Hunt, Jim, *The Men In The Nets* (McGraw-Hill-Ryerson, 1972)

MacPherson, Stewart, *The Mike And I* (Home & Van Thal, 1948)

McFarlane, Brian, *50 Years of Hockey, An Intimate History of the NHL* (Pagurian Press, circa 1970)

Obodiac, Stan, *No Substitute for Victory* (Redeemers Voice, 1952)

O'Brien, Andy, *The Jacques Plante Story* (McGraw-Hill-Ryerson, 1972)

Stanley, A.H., *Raiders Review* (Hockey Publications, 1948)

Thurn, Walter R., *The Famous Bentleys* (Modern Press, 1947)

Vaughan, Richard F., *Hockey* (Whittlesey House, 1939)

Woodley, Richard, *Slap Shot* (Futura, 1977)

The Complete Book of Soccer & Hockey (New York Times, 1980)

The Complete Book of Winter Sports (New York Times, 1980)

The Story of Ice Hockey (Newservice, 1948)

The Nottingham Panthers (Breedon Books, circa 1982)

INDEX